Staying Woke is Killing Me. Vol 2.

Christopher Deans

To Society,

I am both an admire and a critic. I value all that
you are but recognize the flaws that you have.
I love you still.
My heart's desire is your perfection.
My goal is your continuance.
May your legacy show an end of pain and a
concrete example of what equality truly means.

With Love,
-Deans

"I refuse to accept the view that mankind is so tragically bound to the starless midnight of racism and war that the bright daybreak of **peace** and brotherhood can never become a reality."

Dr. Martin Luther King Jr.
Nobel Prize Acceptance Speech
December 10, 1964

<u>PREFACE</u>

Here we are again. Four years later. And Kap still doesn't have an NFL job. Kap out here throwing 60-yard on-target darts. Still has ridiculous athleticism. With half the league's QBs being mediocre at best, and he still is not out there on the field. Discrimination is unrelenting.

Four years later and still, Staying Woke is Killing Me. In the first volume, we defined Oppression. We spoke about the emotional trauma that exists because of it. We spoke about cancel culture and the victimization of being oppressed within society. We learned about systemic discrimination through my experience. I shared my love of basketball and other stories from my journey. We had some laughs too.

At that point, I didn't know the name Jacob Blake, Atatiana Jefferson, Rayshard Brooks and so many more of our brothers and sisters who are no longer with us. I did not fully comprehend the structural mechanisms of oppression that exist within our society. I had less knowledge of how it survives. I was naïve about the historical context of the powerful and how their dominance has a generational legacy. In my time since then, my understanding has grown. Also, I am not laughing any longer.

Thank you for visiting this space. Along this path, we will cover some tough topics. We will get through it together. I promise to handle your experience as a reader with care. Your presence here is valued and I will do all that I can through these pages to make a positive contribution to your journey.

My mother asked me once why I choose to write on oppression and systemic injustice. It's something that I think critically about. Ultimately, I feel that it is a duty. I have an impulse to shine a light on these issues through my writing. It is a calling that I feel in my heart. One in which I follow with intense passion and sincere desire for a better, more equal society.

A commonality that the powerful and the oppressed share is that we are both humans. Once we transcend past the pain and the privilege, at our core we are the same. I lean into that bond with the optimism that one day in addition to what we already share there will be a similarity in our existence and the opportunities that we have along our journey. Until then, I fight.

Chapter 5

Hypocrisy

Do what you say this country is supposed to be about, the land of the free for all. It has not been free for black people and we are tired.
-Tamika Mallory

Growing up, I loved learning about American History. I remember when I was a young child, my mother bought me a placemat for our dinner table that contained all of the U.S. Presidents. To have this placemat was the thrill of a lifetime. I used to stare at that mat each and every night while eating dinner and memorize the presidents, the years they were in office, and so many other facts. To this day, I still have that knowledge memorized. President with the shortest term in office? William Henry Harrison. President after Nixon? Gerald Ford. First president born in Pennsylvania? James Buchanan.

When I got to high school, my love of history continued. I was not the best student and I did not particularly enjoy high school, but history class was always a bright part of my day. Often, I would read the history textbooks even during my other classes. I finished my 9th grade history text in about three weeks. Luckily, I had friends in higher grade levels who were assigned the same lunch period as I, so I would ask to borrow their history text and read during lunch. I could not get enough.

I really enjoyed learning about the accomplishments and triumphs of our country, as well as the way in which we responded in moments of difficulty. I enjoyed reading about FDR's speech after Pearl Harbor and how JFK was able to hold us together on the brink of nuclear war in the Cuban Missile Crisis. Furthermore, I enjoyed that America wasn't perfect, but we had clear morals and principles that we stood for. Through those lessons and textbook pages, I saw a nation that was continually striving and pushing to be better. Those words about striving to form a more perfect union were words that stood out to me all throughout my childhood. It continued to stay with me in adulthood. Above all else, what stood out to me the most was the strength and the resilience of this nation.

Although there are many pieces of American history that I enjoy, my favorite portion is the American Revolution. The courage, the strength, the power, and sacrifice that were displayed around that moment literally gives me goosebumps. The audacity to declare to the world that these new citizens of an American nation are no longer subjects of any king, and have undeniable rights endowed to them by their creator, is powerful beyond measure.

I am able to hold this moment as significant and special in my heart even though at the moment when these events were happening, my ancestors were enslaved to many of those same people who just declared that they themselves were no longer subjects. And in victory, as they began the arduous journey of building a nation, a compromise amongst those same people declared that my ancestors were to be considered just 3/5 of an actual person.

Knowing this, I remind myself that America isn't perfect. Like with a lot of things, there is good and there is bad. But if I were to be honest, in these moments I also feel a deep hurt because of the hypocrisy that these moments represent. The people of this nation were willing to fight and do whatever necessary to win their independence while still holding other people captive themselves. I am repulsed by the idea that bondage was unacceptable to them, but yet should be the standard for people of African descent. However, I try my hardest to check those moments and not let it harden my heart; to look at the full scope and not just a certain set of circumstances that are reprehensible, but do not define the entirety of the movement.

I understand that as humans we are flawed. Man is an imperfect being whose existence is constantly evolving seeking to gain a sense of greater understanding.

Additionally, I understand that slavery was the thinking of its time, and for some they are heavily influenced by their environment. For many, it wasn't absolutely repugnant, it was just a way of life. Obviously, I am not excusing slavers. Their actions were absolutely and unequivocally wrong. I am just simply explaining the counterarguments that I have to tell myself that allow me to continue to cherish the moments of American history that hold a special place in my heart.

This type of dual existence is quite common for many African Americans. In order to celebrate something in our history or to simply just have peace in our hearts, we have to look past the injustice. We are asked, or in many cases we are expected, to agree with or participate in the commonly accepted position or action while not acknowledging the injustice it contains. We are expected to appreciate the public celebration of MLK but not mention the harassment he suffered at the hands of the FBI. We celebrate Crispus Attucks, yet we fail to mention that he was more than likely an escaped slave. We are supposed to welcome Juneteenth celebrations as a new stage of racial equality while not mentioning that the date it signifies was literally two years after the Emancipation Proclamation, more than two years after Lincoln "freed" slaves.

There is a constant expectation that society places on us to look past the injustice and concentrate on the desired point of focus of its choosing. We are asked to do this time and time again, so much so that it has become the expected norm.

Just understand the moment, they are indirectly saying, do not focus on the discrimination that we may or may not have acknowledged as wrong, and focus on the point that we are trying to make.

Forget the harassment; focus on us celebrating MLK as the great man that he was. Forget the fact that slave owners literally signed over their slaves to fight in the Union Army; focus on the fact that the Union was willing to go to war in opposition of slavery and that Lincoln freed the slaves.

Okay, cool. I understand. We should always extend the benefit of the doubt. However, this is where the hypocrisy becomes too much to bear. If it is the desire of society for us to view things from this perspective, why is it so difficult to give the actions of the oppressed that same understanding? For example, why does it seem that public support for Black Lives Matter is always conditional? Why is that perfection is required in all that the organization does? Why does it seem that their efforts are always met with so much ambiguity? Why is it that even after the movement denounced the perpetrators, the narrative about some of their protests then shifted to destruction of property? Why wasn't the focus always on the reason that they were out there protesting in the first place?

As we just discussed, societal expectation is to look past certain things toward the core point of focus, right? To stay focused on the larger picture, correct? So why doesn't society grant the oppressed that same opportunity, that same privilege? Why is the narrative so quickly changed with rhetoric of lawlessness when a Target is set on fire? Burning that Target was wrong, furthermore it was stupid. But why does that shift attention from the fact that the reason that people were out there marching in the first place was because, yet again, a police officer killed an unarmed citizen?

There is a power dynamic at play here that cannot be dismissed. Through its actions, society has shown that certain things are okay for one group and unacceptable for another. To examine this thought, we can examine the history of protests within American society. Disapproval for protests against discrimination is deeply confusing when you factor in this country's history and how it was formed.

The Boston Massacre is widely considered to be the beginning of the American Revolution. During this incident, Boston residents, angered by multiple grievances with the Crown, confronted the English military in a mob mentality on a cold evening in early March 1770.

It is important to note that, by definition, this gathering was not lawful. The crowd had been ordered to disperse; they disobeyed. Furthermore, it was not peaceful. Boston residents swung clubs, threw stones, and threw snowballs at the soldiers. This continued until a soldier was struck by an object, felt provoked and/or threatened, and fired into the crowd.

Despite the circumstances that led up to this horrible evening when Boston residents lost their lives, this event of American history is celebrated as the moment when battle lines were drawn and a nation began to form. Throughout our nation, this moment was a rallying call where the people said, "No more," and took action against British injustice. The slaying of those five individuals sparked a culture of rebellion and organized response, a position that was widely accepted throughout the colonies.

The deaths of those Americans during the Boston Massacre started a war. Yet, when thousands take to the street today to demand justice for brothers and sisters who are murdered while unarmed, the sense of purpose and moral clarity for many seem to fade.

It is confusing to me that so many individuals who hold the slayings of the Boston Massacre as tragic, struggle to feel the same anguish for the many Black individuals who were murdered due to a similar systemic injustice. Individuals who take pride and a patriotic stance in flying the Don't Tread on Me flag, struggle to find the moral conviction to say that Black lives matter.

While considering the morality of all this, it is very important to emphasize that this country was literally founded on a protest. It is also important to emphasize that their actions did not stop there. After the protests, the founders of this nation then took up arms to violently overthrow their oppressors in an effort to win their freedom. Their victory is celebrated every fourth of July when thousands in this country set off fireworks into the sky, an action that is meant to represent the cannon fire that the founders used to win their freedom.

Although I celebrate this moment and revel in the amazing opportunities it gave this nation that I love so very much, it's hard to not acknowledge the hypocrisy that it represents. Those fireworks represent to me, as a Black American, that society has the power to dictate which fight for justice is socially acceptable. American Revolution, Independence Day? Cool. Let's get together and celebrate our nation of freedom and the heroes and sacrifice that it took to create. Black Lives Matter? Well, we agree in premise, but let's talk about the methods being used.

A quote attributed to Winston Churchill says, *"Americans can always be trusted to do the right thing, once all other possibilities are exhausted."*

Watching recent protests, I believed that this may have been one of those moments. As expressed in volume one of this book, I am still a believer in the individual's ability to do good. By and large, it is my belief that the number of individuals who are willing to take positive actions vastly outnumber those who have anger and hate in their heart.

Despite the good I see in people individually, I believe the intentions of people change as a part of larger society. As individuals, people can have the best intention, but as a part of a larger group, behaviors and perspectives change, especially when that group feels threatened. Society has shown us time and time again that those who are in power will do what it takes to protect their own interest. Those in power who feel threatened will bend society to its will to protect their ability to dominate. They will create narratives that paint them in the best light or help to further their agenda of continued domination. They will do so with no regard to the hypocrisy their actions represent and no explanation when their positions change.

For example, let's transition our attention to another time of major military conflict within American History – the Civil War. The Civil War was one of the darkest times our country has ever experienced. This war was an armed conflict where the Southern states of the Union left the Union and declared that they were a free and independent nation.

The war was caused by many different nuanced reasons, most of which are highlighted by slavery in most popular narrative. What is less talked about is that behind the layers was an immense struggle for the way in which the nation would be governed and how it would get to determine its future.

The Southern states believed that they should have more autonomy in the way they are allowed to govern themselves. On certain issues, the Southern states did not desire to defer to federal law. It was their position that their states should have the right to carry out governance how they saw fit within their jurisdiction.

There was also a bitter battle over economics between the North and the South at play as well. The two sides had different economies and different views on what perspective should drive economic activity for the nation.

The Southern economy was an agrarian economy that relied on the production and trade of agricultural products to drive economic activity. The Northern economy was transitioning into largely an industrial economy that used the creation and trade of manufactured goods as a primary economic driver. With rapid industrialization happening in the North, the South saw itself being out outperformed by the North economically. Furthermore, the North's position on certain policies threatened the South's economic future, which brings us back to slavery.

The South's economy depended largely on slavery. The agrarian economy of that time required manual laborers to produce its products to bring to market. The South's economy was able to perform and produce profits because of low production costs due to the fact they did not pay for labor.

With the North's position that slavery should be outlawed throughout the nation, not only would this decision impact the South's way of life, it would also drastically impact their economy. Slavery was indeed a major cause that led to the Civil War, but it wasn't solely a morality issue. There were also issues of the future determinacy of governance and major economic issues that were at play. It is important to the story that we provide full context on what led the nation to war.

The war ended in 1865 with a Union victory but at great cost. The Civil War was one of America's deadliest conflicts; more than 700,000 people lost their lives. A Union victory led to the end of slavery and a period of reconstruction for the nation. The Southern states that left the Union rejoined the Nation, and more than 4 million newly freed former slaves entered a new period of freedom with the majority of those individuals living in the South.

The period after the Civil War is known as Reconstruction. This time in American history is the point in which African Americans had the most political power and the most political representation.

In the years that immediately followed the Civil War, the newly freed slaves created a large voting block that allowed this constituency to send representatives to Congress who would not only look out for their interest but who also looked like them as well. More than 600 African Americans were elected to serve in different positions throughout the nation, 16 of which were elected to seats within the United States Congress.

The sudden loss of political representation, multiple grievances with their defeat in war, and disbandment of the confederacy led to retaliation against the newly freed slaves of the South. Many white individuals used organized violence as voter intimidation to dissuade the newly freed slaves from political participation. These individuals used targeted violence, including murder, to help restore white supremacy that was lost with the sudden change in political fortune. These individuals formed a group that would use violence and terror to reassert their dominance over the black citizens of the South. This group would be called the Ku Klux Klan.

In response to the violence that the Ku Klux Klan was carrying out in the South, the federal government intervened. The United States Congress passed a set of laws called the Enforcement Acts. These laws were created to protect African Americans' rights to vote and hold public office and protect citizens from the terror of the Klan. Furthermore, the Grant Administration sent federal troops into the South to protect black citizens from the violence of the Klan. With the presence of federal troops, African Americans had protection to participate in the political process and continued to do so throughout the Reconstruction Era. However, things would soon change.

The 1876 United States presidential election placed Republican Rutherford B. Hayes against Democrat Samuel J. Tilden. This election was one of the most contentious elections in American history. Although most agreed that Tilden had won the popular vote, there was disagreement regarding the victor of the Electoral College. Tilden had won 184 electoral votes to Hayes' electoral vote total of 165. There were 20 electoral votes that had yet to be decided, with the votes for the states of Florida, Louisiana, South Carolina, and Oregon not being declared to any candidate.

To determine the outcome of the election, the parties established an unwritten agreement that awarded Hayes and the Republicans the presidency. In what will become known as the Hayes Compromise, the Democrats agreed to assign the contested 20 electoral votes to Hayes in exchange for pulling all federal troops from the South when Hayes and his Republican administration were in power. Without the protection of federal troops, this would essentially end the Reconstruction Era in the South. Violence and intimidation once again reigned supreme in the South, and African Americans now saw themselves marginalized from society despite the gains that were made in the years before.

Politically destitute and physically unprotected, black Americans were now relegated to a second-class status that shared similarity to their all-too-recent enslavement. This chain of events created an environment where white supremacy would reign supreme over much of the South for more than 100 years.

As we established earlier, one of the core reasons that the Union claims to have fought the war was for the abolishment of slavery. The Union fought the war to free the slaves. However, as soon as their interests were no longer aligned and their power was at stake, they abandoned the former slaves.

Black Americans were left without political power and without physical protection. They were abandoned knowing all too well what would happen when they were left behind. The same people that the Union had claimed it was going to war to protect were now the people they would be leaving behind to a life of violence and terror. You can't claim to care about a group of people and then abandon them later because it is in your best interest to do so. Things just do not work like that. This is what hypocrisy looks like.

Examples of hypocrisy like this not only anger me, they not only emotionally drain me, but they scare me as well. In the first volume of *Staying Woke is Killing Me*, I talked about how some mechanisms of oppression are deceptive. They operate in the shadows and continue to discreetly perpetuate systemic inequality. Hypocrisy is not that. Hypocrisy is not stealth. Hypocrisy is a blunt force tactic of oppression.

Hypocrisy in its weaponized form is those who have power using that power without any regard to fair or equal treatment. It is done blatantly to impose the will of those who have power to achieve their desired goal. It Is done without any regard to consequence, principle, or past standard. Essentially, I am going to do what I want, when I want, I don't care what you think or say about my actions. I'm doing it anyway.

Obviously, that type of use of power has the ability to crush the morale and spirit of those on the opposite side. Furthermore, the powerless feel like they are trapped in a system of unequal treatment and while some do continuously fight against this reality, others accept their circumstances. They no longer attempt to reasonably address their grievances; they just retreat, repressing their emotions and frustration of their unjust treatment.

Without repercussions to answer to, this continual dominance will be enacted by those with power until the powerless feel that they are no longer able to live under their unjust circumstances. Seeing no other alternative, this ultimately leads to a huge and organized response from the oppressed. It leads to a revolt.

Hypocrisy destroys. It leads to inevitable retaliation and response. The only unknowns are the timing of the response and the level of intensity. Hypocrisy scares me because it is one of the starkest indicators of a system in deep turmoil. It is a flashing red warning light. Additionally, within society it is one of the last stages before opposing voices no longer wish to seek compromise.

This undercurrent can only stay beneath the surface for so long. Eventually it will rise, and you will be forced to deal with it. The unfortunate circumstance is that if you wait, you will be dealing with issues in a midst of mass opposition and conflict. Ideally, you want to call hypocrisy out as wrong and address it as soon as possible. This way those who are suffering do not feel powerless and can see that the actions of oppressors are being labeled as wrong. This provides hope of possible change within society. This also leaves open the possibility for the oppressed to trust that society eventually will create the space for equality. Once equity is gained, we finally may be able to begin the journey to heal.

One of the most important portions of healing is acknowledgement. We must come to terms with the things that were done to us or that we have done to others that cause pain. Only after that happens can we begin the journey of self-exploration to find forgiveness and peace, and move forward in a positive space.

Although we cannot change the past, we are still guided by it. The unfortunate fact is, within our society, our past still haunts us and we refuse to deal with it.

There has been no mutually agreed upon moment in which America has come to terms with the hypocrisy and terror of its past. In fact, in current society, there is actually a war that is being waged about even mentioning it. There are some parts of this country right now that are banning books and eliminating content that seeks to educate the public on these past truths. These individuals are armed with the perspective that these moments in our past should not even be talked about and to do so is unpatriotic and un-American. Reconciliation and contrition for these moments seem like a fairy tale when we are unable to come to terms with speaking about these dark times of our past.

So how can we begin the journey to heal as a society if we are unable to even have the conversation? How can the oppressed begin to mend the wound in their heart that society won't even acknowledge that it caused? How do we trust and try to believe that society has learned and values us as a part of it?

The unfortunate set of circumstances is that until we come to terms with this, we will be unable to truly move forward. Unless we come to terms with the hard truths of our past, we will continue to travel down this descending spiral of strained relations and a lack of social cohesion, especially between the oppressed and the groups of power.

No one is responsible for the actions of their ancestors. It is not rational to hold anyone accountable for the actions of someone before them. However, there is a responsibility to come to terms with what happened in the past and how that has impacted our space in current society. There must be some acknowledgement of what happened and recognition of right and wrong.

Failure to do so damages the credibility of society and hinders our ability to envision a nation without discrimination. How can we expect fairness when society as a whole cannot agree on recognition of past wrongs? Many of us know and fully understand the wrongs of our past, we are just choosing not to deal with them. Choosing not to make amends, but to double down in the egregiousness of the hypocrisy.

Many of these people who are actively banning books that speak to the journey to freedom for Black Americans are the very same people who fought against public health measures during Covid. The main reason for their Covid fight? Freedom, much like the Union and its claims of waging war to end slavery, and then abandoning the former slaves just years later for political power. Hypocrisy is rooted all throughout their actions. Their stance on issues are fluid, yet the hypocrisy that defines their actions is constant.

As painful as their hypocrisy is, it does help to explain the truth behind their actions. These individuals do not fight for causes. That's just the battlefield. They are fighting for power, the fact that it belongs to them and no one else is allowed to have it.

Society has reinforced the idea time and time again that some are destined to have power as if it was gifted to them as their birthright. If they were to ever lose it, they would be batshit crazy in their existence without it, so much so that they must protect and defend it all cost.

As we seen in the South during Reconstruction, this group will resort to whatever tactic it needs to in order to maintain its normalcy of supremacy. Initial tactics will start with misdirection, distraction, and deception, and progress all the way to violence, terror, or murder if necessary, all in the name of maintaining their dominance within society.

With this being the nature of the landscape, it is hard to see this group showing any contrition or remorse for their privilege of power protected by the use of weaponized hypocrisy. Doing so goes against their natural impulse to first protect their own intertest and what society has taught them throughout the years. Packaged within the greatness of all that this nation is and what it has to offer is the idea that we as a people are special, that we are better, that we are exceptional.

The idea of American Exceptionalism has powered this society to achieve things not seen before in the history of the world. Despite the fuel that it provides to motivate us to achieve greatness, it also gives space for a major character flaw in all of us. It can be difficult to see and admit error when you are constantly told how amazing you actually are. When confronted about your error, it can feel like an attack and force you to respond in a manner that is dismissive of the error because you feel the need to defend yourself. The intention of the criticism is not considered, only the feeling that you need to protect yourself and your position.

Admitting failure as an individual is important, but admitting failure as a society is critical. Doing so provides the opportunity for a society to reflect on its actions and evaluate where it went wrong. It creates the opportunity for reflection and growth.

Most acknowledge that many past actions of our nation were wrong. They don't want to talk about them, they don't want to deal with them, but they acknowledge the wrong. Where many struggle now is understanding just exactly what to do with it. How do we address this?

We start by admitting that America is a nation that is based in hypocrisy. We must be strong enough to publicly admit our flaws. We cannot be afraid of the conversation and we cannot be swayed by the discomfort that comes with the acknowledgment of the wrong.

We are a great nation that does many things right, however at our core, we are rooted in hypocrisy. By acknowledging this, it gives us the opportunity to examine our past, think about our future actions, and make different decisions, ones that will hopefully pull society closer together and not tear us further apart.

Because a lot of our issues are structural and systematic, we have a lot of work to do to repair the cracks within our society. But beginning with this simple acknowledgement allows the disenfranchised the opportunity to see a change in society and begin the process of opening their hearts. At this point, maybe the process of healing can begin and we can start to build trust again within society.

Chapter 6

Social Media

The revolution will be tweeted, Instagrammed, Facebooked, it will be recorded.
-Shawnee Benton-Gibson

Patrick Lyoya was killed by a police officer in the early morning on April 4, 2022. I would not be surprised if you did not immediately know the name. The unfortunate fact is that police shootings are so common in our society, I am just not surprised if you are unaware that this young man lost his life at the hands of police. The 26-year-old native of the Congo was traveling in his car when he was stopped by police for his license plate not belonging to the vehicle he was in.

He was instructed by law enforcement to remain in his vehicle. This was a request to which he did not comply. As the incident unfolded, Patrick decided to flee the presence of the officer. The officer gave chase and a struggled ensued. During the struggle, the officer attempted to deploy his taser against Patrick in two circumstances. However, Patrick was not struck by the taser in either circumstance, leaving it ineffective. Toward the conclusion of the struggle, the officer was able to maneuver to a position where he was on top of Patrick while they both struggled. At this point, the officer removed his firearm and shot Patrick in the back of the head at point blank range, ending his life.

After his death, there was debate about Patrick's actions. The rhetoric centered around his unwillingness to comply and that he engaged in a struggle with a law enforcement officer. The uncontrollable sorrow that I feel for Patrick is hard to put into words. Because even though I never met him and I have never shared a word with him, in that moment I shared connection with him that only we who are similar to Patrick can identify with, that dreadful fear that takes over you when you are approached by police as a black male. In that moment, your mind shifts to one place, one thought – Will I leave this scenario alive?

Despite his unwillingness to comply with the officers, despite that there may have been something improper or not correct with his tags, despite that he chose to run, these circumstances do not give the authority to end his life.

Non-compliance should not lead to elimination. I watched this video and my heart broke into a million pieces, and it is still shattered, not healed from all the other brothers and sisters who lost their lives at the hands of police.

It is in this space that I need to be completely honest. I heard about Patrick through a news alert that was sent to my iPhone from *The Washington Post*. When the video was released, I knew it had been made public and released through social media feeds. I had access to it through multiple media outlets. Although I had access to it, I did not watch. Each time I saw it on my feeds, I muted the post. I made the intentional decision not to watch the video. If I am being fully transparent, I did not watch the video until about three weeks later while I was researching material for this book. Up until then, I made the intentional decision to not engage. I stuck my head in the sand. I just could not bring myself to watch.

This was a notable moment for me. It was one of the first clearly recognizable times in my life where I chose to intentionally ignore images and evidence of systemic oppression. I chose to look the other way. One of the core premises of the *Staying Woke is Killing Me* series is to articulate the battle that many of us face inside, the internal war for our spirit. That is, what to do about the oppression that we are surrounded by, how do we respond, and how do we come to terms with it in our lives?

In *Staying Woke is Killing Me* Volume One, I explained that I was at a transitional place in my journey. I was at a place where I was actively trying to decide whether I wanted to continue the fight against oppression or just ignore it.

Fighting a war in which you see constant fatalities is agonizing. Its kills your morale, it murders your spirit. Willfully accepting your oppression and not fighting against it is also agonizing and, from my position, it de-identifies me.

Throughout my life, I have been defined by this fight against oppression. I have been dedicated to this fight. It grounded me. It guided me. It was my North Star and gave me purpose. My mission here on Earth was to fight against oppression to make things better for my community.

Furthermore, it's my belief that I have been able to achieve what I have so far only because of the people who came before me and their willingness to carry this fight. These people never gave up and fought every day of their lives to make my life better. If I was unwilling to make that same sacrifice, what would that say about me? Who was I without this fight?

However, I feel as though there comes a time in every person's life when you can no longer keep going. For many of us, we have times in life when we decide to change the trajectory of our journey. We need to make a different decision because the current choice is not for us any longer. We can no longer operate in the manner in which we once did. With Patrick's story, I was realizing that I may have reached mine. I may have reached the time in my life when I could no longer fight. Learning about what happened to him, I knew this was a circumstance of injustice. I knew what I would see if I watched the video of his murder. I knew how I would feel. It was in that moment that I told myself that I am not watching it. Without any internal struggle, I chose to ignore it. It was as if my heart, mind, and soul all collaborated and said no more. We can no longer absorb these moments of pain.

Our bodies are biologically designed to protect themselves. As humans, we naturally tend to adapt to the elements of our environment. Knowing this, I can make the legitimate argument that the most natural thing for to me to do would be to accept my oppression. It would be just to exist and not take action against it. I could accept the fact that this is the way things are and I am just going to have to learn to live with it.

While making the decision not to engage may be the most natural choice, it is highly unlikely that it would be a decision made of ignorance. It is hard to envision a world where the oppressed are not conscious of their oppression. Regretfully, our lives are surrounded by images of our oppression. In today's society, the main driver of this is a small computer that we carry around with us every day. It's a device that has completely changed our lives and how we exist in them – our cellphone.

Technology has completely revolutionized the way we live our lives. No longer do we just use our phones to make calls, we use them for everything. We use them to connect to the Internet to research information. We use them to navigate us from place to place. We use them to film and capture moments. We use them to socially connect.

The Internet and cell phones have completely re-designed our social experience. Previous versions of our society facilitated relationships and social connections through in-person, face-to-face interactions. The social experience for this version of society has been redesigned so that those old manners of social connection still happen, but they now also happen through the Internet.

At the heart of this technological evolution is the place where social media lives. Social media has revolutionized our socialization process. More common now, the first interaction that you have with a person is not a hello, it's a friend request. People just do not go to and enjoy ball games and vacations at the Grand Canyon any longer. They go to ball games and the Grand Canyon and, on their social media, they share pictures of themselves at the ball game and at the Grand Canyon. Those pictures often include a description of the experience and who they are enjoying that time with. Social media has completely changed the social contract and what is common behavior.

While this evolution has contributed to the progress and added much positivity to our existence, it has also significantly changed things. Our world is a much more connected space now, where almost anything or anyone can be found online. This evolution has created a dynamic where much more of the world is visible now. There were so many things that were happening in the dark that are now happening in the light, more specifically regarding injustice. The cellphone has provided us a way to document and archive evidence of oppression. And social media has provided the platform to amplify this evidence for the world to see.

Will Smith once said, "Racism isn't getting worse, it's getting filmed." For generations, we knew that oppression existed. Yet, time and time again when society was challenged, there always seemed to be some strategic ambiguity in regard to coming to terms with it. The cellphone ended that. In today's society, when these moments happen, there is a high likelihood that the incident is being filmed. And after it is filmed, it will soon be released on some social media site for the world to see.

These images that are released for the world to absorb force society to take note and force each person to process it for themselves. With each image, it provides further context for injustices that we already knew existed. Each video helps to eliminate the probability that an individual has not been exposed to an incident of oppression. These images show clear evidence that our society has a problem, and it needs to be addressed.

Although these images provide documented evidence of injustices that many have been vocalizing for years, they still provide no comfort. At my core, I find it vile and deplorable that society literally has to be shown the destruction of someone's life for it to believe. It is detestable that it needs this evidence for the public sentiment to change, though not entirely, just somewhat.

Going beyond the agony and grief of the victim's family having these images live in the public square for eternity, it's just unfair that we have to witness a member of the community in their most painful moment, a moment from which they will never escape.

Despite my feelings, I have to ask myself a tough question. Without the video, will society truly understand? How do you come to terms with amplifying pain to prove to the world that it exists? There is truly a cruel power dynamic at play when you need to cut your hand to prove to the world that it bleeds. None of this is reasonable, but I rationalize to myself that maybe the burden would be lessened if these incidents were isolated occurrences. However, in our current world, this is the norm. Oppression occupies so many spaces within our society. It is not only violence that is being filmed, there are many more instances of oppression that are being filmed and shown to the world. Images of oppression are available on-demand, and they overpopulate our space. So much so that we are surrounded by them and are unable to have the space needed to truly process them. We are unable to gain perspective, because we are continually surrounded by these experiences.

In warfare, there is a strategy in which soldiers are rotated in and out of spaces where the combat is the heaviest. Traditionally, the area in which fighting is the heaviest is called the "front." Some soldiers are not in these areas for the entirety of their service. In their service, they are switched in and out of locations. This happens for many different strategic reasons. One reason is to provide some temporary reprieve from the violence, danger, and trauma experienced in combat on a day-to-day basis.

I did not serve. Because of this, I am unable to personally speak to the effectiveness of this strategy. However, what I have observed is that many soldiers who serve and are able to leave the battlefield without physical injury, still carry heavy emotional burden.

They carry wounds that sometimes are not easily seen physically yet are very real and will be with them for the rest of their lives. Only someone who has seen what they saw can truly understand and relate to that burden. There are pieces of them left in the place where they served and heroically sacrificed all that they had in service to their nation.

Although I am not able to evaluate from personal experience the effectiveness of this strategy, I want to highlight the forethought and rationale behind it. Multiple levels of military leadership believe that it is a good idea to provide their personnel a reprieve from traumatic situations. By design, they have created a system that takes individuals from trauma and provides them a fresh perspective away from it. Although the emotional burden still lingers, they are not still actively in it and are not constantly reminded by images of it.

Social media and the volume of incidents of oppression have created a dynamic in which we are constantly immersed in our pain. We are unable to get distance and fresh perspective because these incidents are introduced and constantly replayed for us on a consistent basis through social media. When these incidents happen, most of us are introduced to the situation through a video that has been captured and uploaded to social media.

The traditional cycle of these incidents usually happens in the following manner: The incident of oppression happens. This incident is normally first reported by a media source or captured on the cellphone of a person who was present at the time of the incident.

Next, the individual who captured the incident or the media source releases the footage on their social media feed.

The images go viral. Or, if the incident involved police body camera, footage of the incident is released at some point by that public agency with an initial statement of facts. The images are then released to the public and the footage goes viral.

Once the footage is viral, it now lives in the public square forever. Most times when people come across these images, they are just browsing their feeds. They are not actively looking for the incident. They may not even know about it yet. However, they are introduced to it from their social media feed. In many cases, seeing the incident becomes unavoidable. Sometimes the only way to avoid the incident is to unplug entirely.

If it is our desire to stay connected, we are forced to live with the trauma of perpetual racial discrimination. Not only do we have to face the initial trauma of the event, but we are also forced to continue re-living it through continual exposure fueled by social media.

Because of the seamless integration of social media into daily life, oppression is just always there. It is something like a bad dream, replaying over and over again. We are never given the space that we need to heal. We live with this pain as long as we can, until we decide that we are unable to. At that point, we make the decision to try to ignore it, much like I did with Patrick's story.

The only way that we are able to gain the space that we need for our emotional well-being is to disengage completely. However, once we disengage, racism is still the victor because although we made the most natural decision we could, which was to protect ourselves, it comes with the sacrifice of our silence. And in our silence, racism continues forward, with one less person fighting against it.

I have to admit that writing this chapter for me was an extremely nervous experience. For me to release this, I have to accept that these words may open me up to criticism. Although it is not my intent, I fear that some may read these pages and think it unacceptable that I articulated Patrick's story in the way that I did. It's important to me that my reader understands my heart. So know that I pray for him, I pray for his family, I honor his memory. Even though I have never met him, his loss causes me great pain. This is the same for the thousands of other victims of oppression we have lost throughout our history, some whose names we know and others that we do not.

With the state of our current community, the fear that I feel in my process of releasing these words is not without merit. Unfortunately, that fear is a part of another difficult problem. This problem is also largely driven by social media. We live in a society were individuals are often quick to criticize, mock, or vilify. This is coupled with our enhanced ability to connect and communicate. That same cell phone that captures images of our oppression has given us a platform on which we can say and share whatever we desire. It is a megaphone, which we have used to be critical of the things we deem as unacceptable.

This creates a troubling problem that I view as two-fold. First, like myself, people are often nervous when sharing their positions on certain matters. Part of what makes a democratic society work is the ability to freely share one's perspective on the issues. Although this right is protected legally through the constitution, social media has created a societal medium in which people's opinions are now evaluated. Unpopular opinions are often mocked and discredited, and their authors are painted as outcasts.

Along with the criticism of their work, they also have to endure public attacks on their character and how they live their lives. It becomes a campaign of public shaming that puts indescribable pressure on a person who ultimately was just speaking their truth.

Secondly, because of our new enhanced ability to criticize, we are less tolerant of opinions that we do not agree with. There is value in hearing things that you do not like. There is a tremendous opportunity that comes with taking the time to reflect on the thoughts of someone you disagree with. As humans, we have a tendency to defer to the manner in which we see the world. We can be oblivious to the perspective of others because we ourselves do not experience it. Within society, you need dissenting voices to educate others on perspectives not considered and to generate healthy debate within the public discourse.

Within our current reality, however, healthy productive debate has taken a backseat to negative and attacking criticism. More common now is the act of engaging to attack instead of engaging to learn, teach, understand, and grow. Those who are looking for dialogue and commentary to move the conversation forward are often overmatched by those who are there just to prove their point. They seek to prove how right they are and how wrong the people with the opposite viewpoint are. Ultimately this pushes out most of the people who have desire to learn and hear from others, and just leaves the people who are there for the fight.

This behavior is destructive and divisive. Furthermore, it provides incentive for us to stay in our lane and not engage with people who have different experiences than we do. Fear of public shaming and the pain that it causes encourages us to stay in spaces in which our worldview is similar to those in that same space.

We no longer have desire to challenge our own worldview and little desire to seek compromise with those who see things differently. We stay in our own corners because that is a safe space that does not have to deal with public shaming or criticism.

What is even more tragic is that often we are in separate corners on matters that we pretty much agree on in principle. We can agree as a community that incidents of injustice are horrible and need to be responded to.

But often where we differ is the manner in which we respond. This has been a generational challenge for the oppressed. Throughout our history, many have had differing views on response. However, what is new is the intolerance and all-out public attack and rejection of views that are not in complete solidarity with our own.

Largely because of social media, our experience has become so fractured that we are often unable to come to a place of social cohesion about anything, even about how to respond to our own oppression. Heartbreakingly enough, oftentimes the fight about how we should respond becomes the battle that we suit up for and not the war against the oppression itself. Instead, the true opponent does not receive our full attention and continues to dominate because we are unable to address it collectively as a community.

And as that is happening, social media is continually evolving. Over the course of its evolution, it is becoming more and more a collective of platforms of dissent. Designed initially to connect, it has gone off course and dishes out more hurt than it does joy. Although there are spaces and moments where we use it to come together, what is more prevalent now are the moments in which we use it to attack one another. And when we fight, we do so emotionally without any strategic vision. Because these platforms that we use to air our grievances are so accessible, we often easily lean in and act from impulse and not from rational thought.

What cannot be emphasized enough is that the thread that weaves all of this together is pain. The trauma that we experience at multiple levels which is amplified by social media. Knowing this, we have to reconsider our existence on these platforms. We must do our best to not only protect ourselves, but protect the public space as well. As I alluded to earlier, it is not in our best interest to disengage completely.

Despite the pain that will surely be experienced, we should remain visible within these spaces. What I recommend is that we reconsider what our presence looks like on these platforms. We think critically about what we communicate and what we choose to share with the world.

We should eliminate the public rejection of opinions and perspectives that we do not agree with. It is important to address things you think differently about, and it is important to share your perspective on issues. However, we should try our hardest to agree to disagree and not ridicule someone with different viewpoints. As long as individuals remain respectful, we must encourage them to provide their thoughts because their ability to freely share builds trust within the public discourse. That in turn builds trust within the members of society, which is a foundational part of change.

Most importantly, we have to stop using these platforms to fight. It is disorganized and ineffective. Although it is the largest and most accessible platform that we have, it is not the right tool for this fight. Many voices screaming different things does not make any impact. Ultimately, what it breeds is confusion. Many people saying the same thing, however, makes a statement. A community moving forward collectively projects power and strength that will be needed to win this fight. Our actions have to be strategic and have to be full of purpose. They must have the intention of ending oppression and not tearing down the people who are also suffering from it.

Chapter 7

Protest

It is very, very important that we keep control in this moment and we make this as peaceful as possible. We make this as peaceful and as organized as possible. Because you know what guys they want us to mess up. They want us to be disorganized. But not today. Not today!
-John Boyega

Trump was elected president y'all. That shit to this very day still seems so wild to me. Like, for real? I know that anything is possible, but damn. That is who we as a nation chose to lead? That's the direction that we decided to take as a nation after Barack? How did we let this happen?

After Trump was elected, I have to admit, I had a moment. Actually, I had many fucking moments. I am sure that a lot of us did. I was angry, but not at the policies. I understand that different administrations have different perspectives on how to lead. I was not angry at the fact that the Dems lost and the GOP controlled the Presidency, House, and Senate. I was most angry about what Trump represented. The election of Barack Obama brought hope back into the political discourse. What Trump represented was division. He was a person who I thought would drive us apart, not bring us closer together.

So, in response, what did I do? It's probably quite obvious. I lashed out. I was a person who was filled with constant rants and moments of anger. I was pissed off. Everyone who knew me knew that I was pissed off. I was so full of anger that Donald Trump was now our president.

Surprisingly enough, though, I was not angry at first. Initially, after the shock of him actually winning wore of, I tried to take a positive tone. I tried to be optimistic. I told myself and made every effort to enter those next four years with an open heart.

I was going to give him a fair chance. I wrote a very positive post on social media, explaining that he was now our leader and I needed him to do well. His success was our success. The nation needed him to lead and I wished for his success as a leader. I knew that there would be policies and positions that he would take that I would not like; that's part of the game.

Elections have consequences. The winner gets the luxury of setting the table and choosing the direction of the nation for the next four years. However, I wanted him to lead. I wanted him to be a leader for us all, to prioritize all Americans, not just his political base. I wanted him to act in the best interest of the country. I wanted him to take steps for us to come together, not become driven apart. Those were the true desires of my heart. Then, a week into his presidency, comes the Muslim ban.

This nation had horrible atrocities committed to it by people who were Muslim. We, as a nation, will forever feel the wounds and the pain that their evil caused. And we will never forget. However, just because the people who committed those acts of terror and murder against this nation were Muslim, it does not give us the right to condemn an entire religion. The vast majority of people who practice Islam do so in peace. One of the strongest acts of leadership I have ever seen came from a man I strongly disagreed with. But I will never be prouder of an American president than I was when George W. Bush visited the mosque after 9/11. In the company of Islamic clerics, the president said, "The face of terror is not the true faith of Islam. Islam is peace." This is what true leadership looks like. It is a leader making attempts to bring communities together, even in the most painful moments of a nation's history. It is a leader still trying to build us up, not tear us apart.

It felt like Trump's action a week into his presidency was the opposite of what Bush did. He was making clear that certain people would not be welcomed here. He ran a campaign that was pretty divisive, but there was always a hope that he would change course once he was elected. This ban showed us that he had absolutely no intention to do so.

On January 27, 2017, by executive order, President Trump blocked entry of people from Iran, Iraq, Libya, Somalia, Sudan, Syria, and Yemen for at least 90 days.

The rationale that he provided for taking this action was the desire of his administration to prevent foreign terrorists from entering into the United States. The countries from which people were denied entry were nations where Islam was the majority religion. These actions were taken immediately after the order was signed without much diplomatic coordination. And it was pure chaos. There were literally airplanes in the sky with citizens from these nations who would not be able to enter the country once they landed.

Part of the duties of the commander-in-chief is to protect this nation and its citizens from attack. It is up to the president and his administration to ensure that no harm comes to the people under their care. With such a large and critical responsibility, there can be actions that leadership takes that can be overcautious. I understand that. So, as a policy, this action does not make much sense to me, but I yield to the fact that it made sense to them. They are taking action they believe that their duty requires. So, I want to focus my critique, not necessarily on the policy itself, but the manner in which it was rolled out.

Like many times within the Trump presidency, this executive order was rolled out with much showmanship. Meaning, there was a lot of theatre and attention that was being placed on this policy. Trump took multiple opportunities to brag about the order on Twitter. Instead of talking to the American people and trying to explain why his administration thought it was important to take this action, he rolled the policy out as a celebratory and autorotative event. It felt like more of the same policies that he had run his campaign on. He was appealing to the fear in all of us, and communicating, albeit not directly, that Muslims are bad and they should be feared. But no need to worry! He was here to "protect" us from all of them.

Unlike his previous Republican predecessor, Trump made no overtures to the Islamic community. I fully believe that he understood what this executive order would do, the actions that it would provoke within people. Despite this, he made no attempt to decrease the anti-Islamic sentiment. He made no attempt, to just, for a moment, be like a George W. Bush.

It was like all my worst fears of what he could be as a leader were beginning to come true. His path of divisiveness did not stop with the Muslim Ban; this was only the beginning. Throughout his time as a president, he made little attempts to bring us together. With most policies he took, the tweets he sent, I grew more and more furious. So, in that moment, I did what most of us do, I went to my social media page and started sharing my thoughts for the world to see. I had something to say.

For the first year or so of the Trump administration, you would have thought my job was to be a political pundit. I stayed ready so that I did not have to get ready. I was super tuned in to everything that his administration was doing. And with each action, I was ready to share with anyone who viewed my social media my thoughts on what exactly I thought of the action taken and the policy objective. Most of these actions were not favorable in my eyes, so in most posts I was very critical. I explained what the administration was trying to do, why I thought it was a bad idea, and how this action makes Trump bad as a leader. This became my process. It was so normal to me, that when new actions were taken, I did not have any second thoughts. I took notes and prepared a post to share with my followers.

So there came a day when I was having a conversation with someone about my posts. They said that they wanted to share something that I had posted a few weeks ago, but they were having a hard time finding the post. They asked if I would mind searching through my timeline and send them the post directly. I, of course, agreed.

This person asking me to send them a certain post forced me to look through the full gauntlet of my posts. Like the person who asked me to send the post, I had a lot difficulty finding it. At first, I was shocked by the number of posts I had. I had a very high volume of them. I honestly did not realize that I was posting that much. The next thing that hit me was the content. It seemed that I was exclusively sharing about politics. There would be a post here and there about music or sports mixed in, but by and large most of the content that I was creating was about politics, specifically about the criticisms that I had with the Trump administration.

The final thing that hit me, and it hit me the strongest, was the tone of the posts that I was sharing. I was angry. I was condescending. I was elitist. I was reading the things that I was sharing, the words I created for the world to see and those words painted a picture of a person that I could not recognize. What I was sharing was not the person that I am. What I was sharing was who I would not want to meet. A person who, in their own way, was divisive, with no intention of bringing us closer together. Through my anger, I became everything that I was fighting against.

When I came to this realization, I was so disappointed. I thought of the people who read my content. What were their thoughts? I thought of the people who may have considered my page a safe space for knowledge, positive energy, and for dialogue. I know that I did not represent that. Those words were of a person who was building walls, not bridges. Through negative and critical commentary, I was in my own way, pushing us further and further away. And above all else, I felt ashamed. Embarrassed. I was better than this. I was absolutely playing myself.

Looking at my content, I realized that no one would take me seriously. What can you gain from someone who is just constantly screaming on social media? And everything they share is just a different version of the same thing. Furthermore, in my anger, I lost my ability to be considered objective. Reading my content, I felt the same vibe as Trump with his Muslim ban. Instead of Islam, it was Trump. Trump is bad. Trump is stupid. Trump is not a good person. Here are all the reasons why.

Looking at my actions, I realized that I needed to make a change. So, I took a step back. I took a moment to think critically about how to move forward. Sharing on social media in constant outrage was not going to get me anywhere. This was not going to change a thing. Moreover, it was diminishing my credibility as a leader. I needed to take a different approach. I needed to do something real.

I see so many individuals who are in that same space that I was. They are traveling along that same path, taking those same actions, falling into that same cycle of sharing anger and frustration through social media. As a community, I think it is time that we take a different approach. Collectively, we need to take meaningful action that will help us move the community forward. That means making sure our protests are grounded in strategy instead of emotion. It requires making sure that the moves we make are calculated and designed to have the greatest impact. We need to ensure that our presence is felt and that with our protests, we can create real change with our actions. What follows next are some thoughts on how we as a community can make that happen.

Examine.

One of the first things that we need to do as we start this journey is to soul search. We have to examine our hearts and come to terms with how we all truly feel. Everyone's process will be different. We all will feel different things, discover different feelings along this path. I can only speak of my experience. I think initially, there had to be some acknowledgement of the pain. Society has inflicted years and years of pain on our community. For me, I used to constantly minimize it and not take it as the serious problem that it is.

Part of my previous journey was to repress the things that I felt and not deal with them because I didn't consider them to be a big deal. I was conditioned to believe that showing emotion, especially as a black man, was a sign of weakness. I needed to be strong, no matter what was presented to me. So, no matter what came my way, I tried my hardest to remain strong. I did not give myself the opportunity to feel. I became numb to a lot of things. Because of this, my soul was filled with anger just waiting for the target on which it could be released and directed toward.

Before I looked at my social media posts, I would not say that I was an angry person. My perception was that I was a pleasant and very chill person. It wasn't until I saw those words, my own content, that I came to terms with the anger in my heart. Trump was the outlet, but he was not the source of this anger that I was filled with. This came from a much deeper place. I had to go on a process of self-discovery to understand the reason for my anger and how it was playing out in my life.

Through this process, I was able to understand that what I have been feeling I had been feeling for years. So much so, that when certain things happened throughout my experience, that automatically triggered a certain response.

Through this journey, I was able to realize that I was indeed angry with the things that the Trump administration was doing. However, what truly triggered me was the powerful hurting those who are weaker. More simply, bullies.

Bullies are my trigger. To this day, if I witness someone being bullied, I have an intense emotional response. I am instantly filled with passion and aggression ready to do whatever necessary to defend against the bully. This comes from my childhood experiences of being viciously bullied through my younger years. It is as if something snapped in me as a grew older and said, "No longer." I will no longer tolerate bullies. I am prepared to do whatever it takes to eliminate the power they have over me and anyone else.

I had to come to terms with that. THERAPY WAS CRITICAL! I think that therapy is amazing and should be a part of everyone's journey. However, it was very important for me to come to terms with what I was feeling in my experience because those feelings were guiding the actions that I was taking. It is very important that we all recognize that. We have to do this work, to comes to terms with our emotions because they guide our actions.

And without this examination process, we will not be able to do what it required moving forward. I know there is a collective pain felt by many who share my experience. Much like I am, many others are angry. I chose to show my anger through social media, others can choose to showcase their anger using different methods. If we allow it, that anger can drive our emotions to a response that includes violence and destruction. We must resist this at all costs.

One of the core things that we have to do when we examine our hearts is to surrender our capacity to respond with violence. We have to surrender any desire to respond with destructive measures. We will not progress our cause through destructive means.

These actions are guided by vengeance and retaliation and will not help us move forward. What they allow is for the opposition to frame us as a threat that is out to hurt and destroy them. Responding with violence gives them the moral license to continue the same actions of oppression that we are fighting against.

Moreover, it provides a distraction that the powerful can focus on instead of the core parts of the injustice. We want the primary focus to stay on the injustice. The methods of resistance are going to generate interest in the cause. So, whatever actions are taken to fight against the oppression have to remain moral. They have to remain ethical. These actions must draw people in, not push people away. People can see themselves peacefully marching. That is a movement that individuals would want to be a part of. And part of the goal is to add as many people as possible to the cause. The desire to join will change when we are looting and burning supermarkets or throwing rocks at police officers. This takes away from what we want to accomplish.

As we examine our hearts, essentially what we have to do is come to terms with taking the high road. This may be difficult, and I understand. However, it is what is required. The eye for an eye response won't work in this circumstance, not with this. Returning violence with violence, destruction with destruction will only contribute more darkness, more pain, and that is not what we are setting out to do. As a community, we cannot have a mission of gaining equality by using pain and destruction to accomplish that goal.

Define.

What is our goal? What are we looking to achieve? These have to be core questions that guide our protest movement. As we have talked about, actions that we take in this fight should be strategic.

They must contain purpose and be actions that are well thought out. Many actions that are taken in response to oppression are impulsive. It makes sense that people would act off of impulse because oppression is a visceral, emotional experience. To the person who is subject to it, it does not feel great. A natural response would be to immediately take action against it. That is not the route that we have to choose. We have to put strategy into our actions. Part of that strategy is thinking about what we want to achieve.

Action without thought is wasted energy. It is not in our best interest to act until we know what we are looking to accomplish. We have to have clear, targeted goals that guide our protest. What are we looking for and what will it look like once we accomplish that goal? Furthermore, how will accomplishing that goal help to end the injustice within society?

Acting in this manner will allow us to focus on certain goals and prioritize what it will take to accomplish them. All of our actions in that moment should be used to rally around accomplishing this goal. Only after we accomplish that goal do we allow ourselves to move forward to the next goal. Whatever we have just accomplished, we are able to use that as a building block to move forward to our next goal. This process allows us to move forward in a clear, concise, and structured way. Additionally, it allows us to see tangible progress of what we have been able to accomplish. We can then use that to show others the work we are doing and the progress that has been made. This gives us additional opportunity to recruit others using these achievements and gain new allies in our fight. What is commonly happening is that members of our coalition are acting without much strategic planning.

They have the best intentions, but people are just acting in the best manner they know how, with whatever means make sense to them. While taken with the best of intentions, this is often ineffective because we have multiple members of the community, working on multiple things instead of joining efforts and working on things as a collective unit. And when members do act, it tends to address whatever incident of oppression that is most prevalent at the time.

For example, there was an incident that happened in 2018 where two black men were arrested as they were waiting for a business partner for a meeting in a Starbucks in Philadelphia. The gentlemen asked the store to use the restroom despite not ordering anything. Store employees asked the gentlemen to leave soon afterward. The gentlemen declined to leave the establishment because they were waiting on a third party. The manager of the store thought this behavior warranted a call to law enforcement. She called the police within minutes of their initial arrival to the store. When the cops arrived, the two gentlemen were arrested. The two young men were actually real estate developers and were meeting at the coffee shop to discuss their next project. But they were also young black males, whose presence represented a threat in the eyes of that manager, a threat that needed to be removed.

Of course, there was video of the gentleman being arrested. The image was shared via social media and the story went viral. (We previously discussed how this cycle normally goes.) As news of the incident spread throughout the country, people were obviously upset and wanted to respond to the incident.

Some of the most immediate responses were activists protesting inside the business. After that happened, community members began to protest outside the building. Some took to social media to voice their anger with the situation.

Through social media, some called for a complete boycott of Starbucks products. There were multiple forms of resistance that were taken by the community.

Although I understand all the actions taken in response, I have to question what were the goals of the protests? Was the goal to show the nation that we were pissed off that things like this keep happening? If so, that was accomplished. But beyond that, what did we accomplish with these actions. In these moments, what did our protest represent?

After the incident, Starbucks went into immediate damage control and fix-it mode. Their CEO flew out to Philadelphia to meet with the gentlemen. The company closed their stores nationwide for a racial sensitivity training. And the company made amends personally to the two gentlemen who were arrested.

Although the company seemed sincere in their remorse, we have to acknowledge that ultimately, they are a business. At the end of the day, they have a brand and a bottom line to protect. When they are allowed to define the terms, they are going to take actions that are in their best interest. What we need to do in moments like this is to join together and create movements that challenge organizations like Starbucks.

We set and create targeted goals that we would like to achieve and attach those to our movement. So whatever action we take, whether it's a protest outside the store, disruption to their supply chain, or a national boycott, we do it together. And we set the terms on what we want to see happen to end the action.

Those goals should be measurable and designed to create change within the spaces where the injustice happened. Racial sensitivity trainings are cool, but what would be more impactful is increased diversity among franchisees and store leadership.

The more diverse spaces are, the more diversity in ownership and in leadership, the less fearful spaces will be when diverse individuals enter the space.

Community leadership did a good job taking this approach in response to incidents of racial injustice in 2020. There were some impromptu protests and some incidents of rioting and destruction of property. However, for the most part, a lot of the actions that were taken were coordinated. Marches were coordinated not only here in America, but throughout the world. There were millions of people marching together, all showing a united front.

It also went beyond the protesting. Community leadership thought about the things that we would like to see happen to end police brutality and end the unjust murders of citizens at the hands of police. They were able to use these ideas and these discussions to create legislation that they would take before Congress.

From the protests of 2020 came the George Floyd Justice in Policing Act of 2021. The bill would give the Justice Department subpoena power to mandate compliance with pattern or practice investigations of departments with suspected bias or misconduct. It would establish a national registry for police misconduct. It would mandate that all federal police officers wear body cameras. The bill contains many other critical things that would directly address the issue of police brutality. The bill actually became stalled in the Senate after the House passed it in early 2021. Despite the eventual deadlock in the Senate, this was an example of the steps we should be taking. We have to set clear goals that we are looking to achieve before we choose to act.

Organize.

This is where things can get really interesting. In order for any action that we take to have the greatest level of effectiveness, we need to organize as a community.

In other words, we need to come together. There can be challenges that arise when communities try to unify because many of us view these issues differently. Although we understand and agree that injustice needs to be eliminated, we differ on ways to respond. There is a lot of possibility depending upon the manner in which we choose to act in response to injustice. We have a lot of different options at our disposal. As long as the actions taken are not violent or destructive, we have a wide array of opportunity.

However, we need to be smart about this. As varied as our options are, we need to counter-balance that with targeted action. As previously said, we need larger coalitions to have the maximum level of effectiveness. We could have a community that passionately pushes back against oppression, in a collective of hundreds of groups filled with a handful of people, each group having a different manner in which they respond. Or we could have a handful of groups, with hundreds and thousands of people that respond in fewer but targeted ways. I can see the merit with both approaches. However, the ladder provides us with strength in numbers and provides a more organized and deliberate response. And it allows us to move forward in a more strategic way. Once we accomplish one goal as a community, we can move on to the next, progressing our agenda at each step of the journey.

With this, it will be important to join groups that best align with your viewpoint. With multiple opportunities available, you have the ability to join spaces that make the most sense to you. It is important that you not only are passionate about ending the injustice, you have to be aligned with the manner in which you are resisting.
It is hard to dedicate the passion and energy that you will need for a cause if you do not agree with the vision of the organization supporting that cause.

As with much in this journey, consolidating into fewer groups will take sacrifice. First, it means the loss of personal visibility. As we talked about in the Social Media chapter, we have an incredible opportunity of visibility in this current climate. Our cellphones and social media provide us with the opportunity to create our own movement without much organizational structuring. We can pretty much share what we want to with the entire world. And we are the individual who gets the recognition for the content, not the organization that we represent. When we concentrate our power and join these groups, we no longer have the visibility that we once had. Now when we speak, the organization has the largest name recognition, not ourselves.

We also sacrifice control. Acting individually, you have the space to do whatever you want. You solely are in control. However, within a smaller group, you have greater opportunity to influence the group to take actions that you desire, to influence members to see things from your perspective. That influence gets smaller when you join larger groups. More than likely, your group would function similar to a democracy where leaders are selected to represent the organization and its' interest. Decisions for the organization are voted upon and the majority decides. Within this type of group, you have power, but not complete autonomy.

To join these spaces, we must accept that we play a small role within a larger team. The interest of the group comes before our own personal agenda. These are all large sacrifices indeed, but the returns that we receive on these sacrifices will be more than generous. Not only will these steps amplify our voices, it will extend our reach and our ability to impact society.

It's kind of ironic. By stepping back and joining larger teams, what we believe in, what we communicate, and how we act, will have a louder and stronger voice. One with clarity, a clear purpose, and more power than we had in our smaller collectives.

We have the ability to create these spaces and to create these groups in which we would concentrate our power. This should be done from time to time to ensure spaces evolve as society moves forward and as our coalition grows. However, we have to be mindful not to dilute group representation too much from other organizations because then we harm their effectiveness. However, I think our best option would be to join the existing infrastructure of groups who already are doing the work. Connect with community groups that have a track record of being active. Join groups who have a mission we already believe in.

My first year of college, in my spare time, I mostly hung with my friends, went to the mall, and played NBA2K. It was not until the second semester of my sophomore year that I started to grow intellectually, generating an interest to get involved on campus and in the community. As I was learning more and more about the challenges in the community, I felt a deeper and stronger urge to help. I felt that I needed to get involved.

Filled with passion, I charged into my mentor's office and told him about an organization that I wanted to create. It would be a campus organization that would be dedicated to helping provide support programming to local inner-city youth.

My mentor replied that he was happy that I had these ideas, and he thought that type of program would work well in the Central Pennsylvania community in which I went to school. He then said that if creating an organization was really what I wanted to do, that he would help me every step of the way. However, he asked me had I considered joining the Black Student Union. Until that moment, I had not.

He explained to me that there was value in creating something from the ground up. He respected it. But he thought that I could have a lot of success joining the BSU and bringing those ideas to that organization. He explained that when creating an organization, it takes a lot to build the infrastructure and begin to network and do many other start-up tasks. When joining an established organization, however, I could benefit from the legacy and infrastructure that was already there. A lot of the contacts that I needed to make this program happen, they already had. Using the BSU's existing contacts, I could dedicate my energy to making the program successful, not building the organization up. And my presence would be very beneficial to the BSU because the organization would get some new blood with new perspectives and ideas.

I learned an important lesson from my mentor that day. I took his advice and I joined the BSU. The program that we were able to create was more impactful as a part of the BSU. Additionally, I had so much more support than I would have just doing it on my own. We were able to also collaborate with other organizations outside of the Central Pa. region. So we were able to expand our reach and touch more students. I was able to accomplish my goal in a more effective manner by joining the BSU.

In this work against injustice, there are already groups who are out doing the work. There are college organizations like the one that I joined. There are national organizations like the NAACP, the ACLU, and the National Action Network. There are also newer groups that have been established as society has evolved, such as Black Lives Matter and Indivisible, who have the infrastructure and the capacity to create real change.

Synchronize.

So imagine that you are home watching your favorite sitcom. And the star of the show delivers a joke. And the joke is hilarious, so funny that you have tears in your eyes. Now imagine that you happen to stumble across that same show a few months later and you watch that same episode. When you hear the joke again, it makes you laugh, but it is not as funny as it was the first time that you heard it. When you hear it for a third time, more than likely it will not be funny at all anymore. If you were to hear it again, you probably will not emotionally react to it all. This is because messages lose their emotional impact over time. The more times we hear something, the more our emotional capacity diminishes over what we just heard. Those initial moments are so valuable because that is the space in which we can have the greatest emotional impact. It is vital that we take full advantage of this.

As we move forward, it is important that we are strategic about the ways in which we communicate. Part of this strategy would be to consolidate and synchronize our communication.

One of the core reasons we need to do so would be to allow us to speak with a unified voice. That voice can communicate with clarity and with strength. Our communication, the messages we share with society, is one of the greatest resources that we have at our disposal. Knowing this, we have to protect it and use it only in ways that make the most sense. We must use it in ways that further our causes, not ways that are impulsive or cause confusion.

This starts with being intentional and thinking critically about what we share on social media. Ideally, when it comes to matters regarding injustice, your posts should have a strategy. The content that we post represents us as a person. These social media profiles live in the public square.

What we share in these spaces will represent us as the type of individual that we are to the public at large. Society will judge us based on what we share without knowing us personally. It is important that we are conscious about what we share and understand how that will represent us a person. Much like I learned from my experiences posting about Trump, if we are not careful about what we share, it will portray an image of us that is not who we are.

One of the benefits that we have from being a part of an organization is that everyone has their own roles. Within our groups we are able to identify individuals who fit into certain spots based of their talents and skillsets. One of the most important roles within the group is the person selected to serve as the communicator. This person, whomever they may be, should be the person who speaks for the group. Things can get messy and chaotic if all members of the group choose to communicate in whatever manner they select. However, if the group is able to come together and select one member who will serve as the primary communicator, this will provide clarity and structure. Also, it gives the group the opportunity to think critically about what it would like to share and strategize about the correct manner in which to do so.

It would make sense if the people who are communicating on behalf of the group are individuals with name recognition and stature within the community. This could be an elected official, community leader, educator, faith leader, activist, business leader, or other individual who is already in the community doing acts of service. It is important that we select this person wisely, because their presence will become intertwined with the organization. This person should be someone with integrity and credibility as they will become the voice of the organization. If they are not credible, the messages shared will not be viewed in the manner needed for them to have any effectiveness. The content of the organization will no longer be the point of focus; it will be the person who is sharing the message.

Synchronizing our communication also provides us the opportunity to own the messaging. We discussed in Volume One that one of the tricks of oppression is to distract and misdirect. With multiple individual communicators, this provides society with more opportunity to distort what one person is saying, paint it as divisive, and cast that onto the entire movement. Society does this in an attempt to find anything that can be picked apart to distract from the core message, which is the highlighting of injustice. By limiting who communicates and vetting what they share, we are able to anticipate these tactics and create contingency planning for when an attack on our messaging inevitably happens. We will know how to pivot and move forward with counter-messaging that pushes back on the distraction.

Additionally, we are able to coordinate our messages with other groups to maximize effectiveness. It would not make sense if different groups are stepping on the messages of groups that they are working with.

Coordinating our messages gives us the opportunity to think about what messages make sense for which demographics and what type of communication should be shared to appeal to those groups. For example, let's say that as a community we made the decision to focus on voting rights. The NAACP and the National Action Network could take the lead on canvassing communities and doing direct engagement through community events speaking about voting rights. Meanwhile, BLM could take the lead on social media and podcasts that spread the voting rights message through the Internet. Multiple organizations, using different forms of messaging, focused on the same issue, communicating in a unified voice. Synchronizing gives us the opportunity to amplify our voices while providing a clear unified message that gives us the chance to have the greatest impact.

Action.

There are two main things that drive this nation's ability to be a world superpower – our military power and our economic power. When we talk about this idea of the ruling class, wealth plays a huge part in this. Power is concentrated with those who have the most wealth. Their wealth provides opportunity and access that many others are unable to acquire. It is important to keep that in mind as a community when we push back against oppression.

When we are considering our protest movements, we have to take actions that are designed to have the maximum level of impact. What can we do? What actions can we take that will really cause society to pay attention?

I have always been of the opinion that in a capitalist society, it's not speeches and marches that get the highest level of attention.

What truly captures this nation's attention is the fucking money. Impact someone's bottom line and you will have their full attention.

When we protest, we should do so non-violently with economic disruption in mind. We have to focus our efforts and actions on methods that structurally target commerce and services. These efforts should be sustained protest efforts that shake the foundation of companies and individuals to cause turmoil in their markets. If we are successful with these efforts, we will have an opportunity to have significant impact and influence actions that create change.

Like I previously said, if we do this correctly, we will have society's full attention. There may be an opportunity to change some hearts once people hear and understand the reasons that we are taking the actions that we are. And honestly speaking, even if they do not understand where we are coming from and do not agree with our positions, they still will be incentivized to join our cause to end the protest.

The protest that we engage in is a threat to the health of their business. Key stakeholders will do what it takes to protect their businesses. I am sure that Starbucks had the best intentions when they took the actions that they did after the Philadelphia incident. But make no mistake, they were getting out in front of a potential massive protest response that would have been caused by this incident of discrimination. The last thing they wanted or needed was a national boycott of their products. That would have been detrimental to their business. So, they took action, immediately.

History has shown us examples of how to do this, of how to engage in this type of protest. Much of the world was introduced to Martin Luther King Jr. through the Montgomery bus boycotts in the mid 1950s. The Montgomery bus boycotts started in December 1955 when Rosa Parks, a secretary of the NAACP, refused to give up her seat to a white patron. In response, a coordinated protest movement was launched to end racial discrimination within public transportation.

What made this protest successful was the unity and buy-in from the community, and the huge economic impact that it had. At the time of the bus boycotts, the vast majority of people who used the public transit system were African American. When African Americans stopped using the system, the transit lines swiftly lost their consumer base for its services. Overnight, close to 70% of their customers refused to use their services. In order to not ride the buses, people carpooled, took taxis, used bicycles, walked, and found any other method of transportation other than the buses. During the boycott, the transit system lost between 30,000 to 40,000 fares a day. This had a drastic economic impact on the transit system and on the local government that ran the transit company. Not only was the transit business impacted, so were the companies that counted on the bus service to transport customers to their businesses. The protest had major economic implications for the entire Montgomery economy.

In response to the police killing of Jamar Clark in Minneapolis in 2015, Black Lives Matter had one of the most effective protests that I have studied in recent history.
Two days before the 2015 Christmas holiday, BLM launched coordinated protests at two epicenters of commerce inside the Minneapolis metropolitan area.

First, protesters blocked the roadway access to one of the busiest terminals at one of the nation's busiest airports on one of the busiest travel days of the year. Simultaneously, they protested and disrupted operations at the nation's largest mall during one of the busiest shopping days of the year. Both protests caused mass disruption and overwhelming confusion during vital moments for both of these sectors.

These protests were brilliant. They were exactly what we should be doing, non-violent, coordinated, highly disruptive, and highly effective demonstrations.

In Montgomery, the community realized the strength of their purchasing power. As a consumer, we have the right to spend our money in spaces where we are treated fairly. When we as a community make up the majority of the patronage of that business, this provides us with overwhelming power. If we join together, we have the ability to dictate the terms. If those terms are not met, we can pull our business. And when we do so, no company can survive that. It is impossible for a company to lose the majority of its business overnight and remain profitable.

In Minneapolis, this showed a level of evolution with our protest movements. It is one thing to have peaceful marches throughout the streets in support of a cause. That's great. But it is another thing to have protests that cause mass economic disruption within trade and commerce. These protests were brilliantly targeted at the structural infrastructure of two major economic hubs for our economy.

And they were conducted at their busiest times.

Now imagine if we were to amplify that. Imagine if next year the same thing happened, but this time it did not just take place in Minneapolis. Imagine if there were also demonstrations in the malls and airports of Los Angeles, New York, Atlanta, Charlotte, Miami, and Dallas. Some of the busiest airports in the world and some of the largest financial centers on the globe.

All experiencing demonstrations, all of which are coordinated to happen at the moment of maximum impact. These types of protests could really have a sustained impact. And we use that impact to create real substantive change.

The final piece of this happens politically. And as much as I hate to admit this, money drives politics. If you are interested to know the priorities of an elected official, look at the entities that are supporting them financially, the people or organizations that are contributing to their political organization.

Admittedly, I hate this. I hate that money is involved in politics at all. However, we have to accept that money is needed for politicians. It is used to help fund their campaign so that they are able to run and win political office. Organizations financially support politicians who support their causes. They want these people to be elected so that when they are in office, they will be there to represent their interest. This is a space in which we need to drastically increase our participation. We need to fund candidates who can speak for us politically. We need to be a major funding source for candidates who are seeking elected office.

In the current political climate, small dollar donations are just as important as large sum political donations. Small dollar contributions direct from citizens are creating new funding opportunities that have been very impactful for politicians and their campaigns.

Part of what makes the Trump and MAGA movement so powerful is their ability to fundraise. They are able to generate millions through thousands of small dollar donations from the community in which supports them.

In our groups, we should consider fundraising campaigns that direct our members to contribute to candidates that we identify. If we are able to raise enough to make a sizable impact, this will gain the attention of the political community. That matters. In politics, money drives results. Money means support and long-term viability. Our donations will make our allies politically stronger. The greater our contributing strength, the more we are able to find and fund additional candidates that we can support to represent our causes. The more political representation we have, the greater our opportunity to create meaningful legislation that creates change.

Political Compromise.

The political landscape has changed drastically since the election of Barack Obama. Since the election of 2008, the country has become more and more partisan. As a nation, moderates are becoming more and more isolated as more of the country's political ideologies are becoming more extreme. Political ideologies that at one point would have been considered too extreme are now becoming mainstream. This hardline ideology is happening on both sides, on the left and on the right.

Even though the election of Barack Obama was a wave election where Democrats won the House, Senate, and Presidency, his opponent in that election still won a large percentage of the vote. John McCain, the Republican nominee in the presidential election of 2008, earned just short of 60 million votes.

This amounted to more than about 46% of the total vote share. Even though Senator McCain won so many votes, he still lost in a landslide. This is in thanks to the Electoral College. We will talk more about the Electoral College in a moment.

President Obama was able to beat Sen. McCain in the electoral college, 365 to 173. In terms of presidential elections, this was a wide margin. The election before this one in 2004, President Bush beat Sen. John Kerry by only a margin of 35 electoral votes. The election of 2000, in which Bush faced Gore, was one of the most controversial in history. Bush won only by 5 votes. Occasionally there are outliers, but by and large, most presidential elections are somewhat close battles in terms of the Electoral College.

Presidential races are often close because they are national elections. And as a nation, most of the views of our citizens align close to the center. Well, at least they did at one point. In political terms, these individuals whose views are in the center are called moderates. And because moderates at one point made up the majority in both parties, national politics was defined by the center. Throughout our history, politicians who were able to do well nationally were those of moderate voices. The goal of national candidates in most elections is, after they win their primary, to add as many votes to their coalition as possible. They achieve this by being moderate enough to gain votes from the other side.

What is happening now in our evolving political system is that moderate voices are being pushed out. These voices are beginning to be cannibalized by the voices in their party that are more extreme. For both conservative and liberal voices, the center is more and more becoming the place where it is harder to find traction. Without broad support in the middle, leaders are forced to align themselves with the positions and ideology that has the majority – the extreme.

As a part of our foundational principles, citizens have the right to rally in support of whatever political ideology makes the most sense to them. This country has been defined by this difference of opinion about how government should operate. But in those differences, our system is designed for its members to seek compromise and respect the view of the opposition. What is happening now, however, is the popularity of more and more extreme voices is pushing us further away from one another. Our positions are so far from the center and are becoming held by so many, it is harder for us to come together. This is coupled with the toxic environment of us becoming increasingly less tolerant of the other party's positions.

Throughout our history, we have looked at the other side of the aisle as the loyal opposition. We have viewed our political party opposition as a group of individuals with different ideas about governing the nation, but groups that are needed for the success of the country.

More and more, our parties are looking at one another as opponents and as groups that must be dominated in all matters. And in this quest to dominate, this brings us back to a common theme – the desire for power.

Political parties actively fight for their ability to acquire, hold on to, and concentrate power. The parties view this fight for power as their primary objective instead of the ways they could use that power to serve all Americans. While fighting, both parties have tried to create structural advantages that allow their reign on power to continue forward into the foreseeable future. However, these tactics have created great peril within our system and given space for many to question the integrity of our democracy.

Within a democracy, it should be that the voters are able to select their representatives. Candidates campaign for office representing a certain community, and the voters of that community select the candidates that they would like to see in office.

However, what would happen if a party was able to influence this process? What would it look like if the only people that voted in a community were the people who have similar views? And what if those communities with individuals with certain views were the majority of the spaces that needed representation?

By law, the federal government of the United States is required to count every citizen living within the country. This process is called the census. The census determines the political representation of the nation moving forward for the next ten years.

So, for example, let's say that you lived in a state called Anywhere, USA. Before the last census, your state had two senators, which every state has, and eight House representatives. Your House representatives are based on the number of people living in your state. And each of the representatives serve one of eight districts that your state has been divided into. Remember this part; it is critical to what is happening.

So then, let's say there was a recent census and it shows that your state had significant population growth. So much so, that your state will now gain two additional representatives, increasing the total amount that it has from eight to 10. To accommodate these additional representatives, the district lines must be redrawn to represent 10 districts instead of eight. This process is called redistricting. If you are creative enough and have the will power to do so, the authority that controls the redistricting process can create a strategic advantage for the party of their choice.

Within our nation, certain areas tend to have certain political tendencies. For example, many urban population centers tend to have a high concentration of Democratic voters. Rural areas tend to have a higher number of Republican voters.

If you can concentrate many democratic voters into one or two districts, that can give you a huge advantage politically. Even though a large percentage of the population in your state lives in these urban population centers, they are only represented by a couple elected officials.

Meanwhile, the other eight districts that tend to be Republican, have way less population but more political representation. Districts can also be redrawn where just small portions of a large mostly democratic urban center are included in multiple congressional districts. There could be parts of an urban center that is carved up into four or five districts to dilute the impact of a larger population.

So even though the urban center is large, the districts that represent it will still have a majority of Republican voters because only a small part of it is included in each district. These types of tactics are called gerrymandering and it is poisoning our political process.

Both parties have engaged in gerrymandering to maintain their political supremacy. This gerrymandering is fueling the movement that is pushing out moderates. Districts that often change representation between the Democratic or Republican candidate as their representative are called swing districts. Swing districts are becoming less and less common. What is more common now are districts that are solidly Democratic or solidly Republican. These districts that are solid blue or red give politicians the political capital to go further to the left or to the right. In a quest to achieve more votes, their views are becoming more and more hardline to appear more conservative or progressive. Simultaneously, these individuals are less willing to work with their opposition when elected as a display of the strong conviction of their political beliefs.

As we talked about in the Social Media chapter, democracies are in desperate need of dissenting voices. We need voices of opposition to push the narrative forward and allow us to hear from the other side on the issues.

The politicians on the other side represent citizens just like our representative represents us. We must respect their positions and understand that while they have a different view from you, they still play an important role. Viewing things from this perspective gives the opportunity to collaborate and work together for the greater good of the nation. Regrettably, this is not happening within our current system.

What scares me now is that we are approaching a moment where we are no longer able to govern among one another. Political parties are looking to dominate the other side instead of finding ways to compromise and come together.

Although the political climate feels more divisive, it is important to remember that despite the rise of the political extreme, we still have common ground politically. The extreme is on the rise, but it has not overtaken the majority of the nation as of yet.

I do believe that this extremism is winning inside the political parties, but the nation as a whole is still moderate. For the time being, we are still a country that is defined by the middle. It is important for us to act while we still can. While I do believe that the system is in trouble, I still believe that we have time to fix it. What is growing is a cancer inside the heart of our democracy. We have to get to it and cut it out before it destroys us.

What we need to do is create a change in the system that forces us to politically compromise. That is what the framers intended when they designed our current system of governance. The founding fathers created a system in which the government would operate in a space of checks and balances.

There would be three equal branches of government where no branch has complete control and the public would have the power to elect the representatives of these branches.

A brilliant system in its creation, the system has become vulnerable as the country has evolved in a way that the framers could not anticipate. The influence of political parties, political media coverage, and political contributions have revolutionized our system in a way that has been detrimental to compromise. We have to shift the dynamic back to encourage compromise.

This is where we circle back around to the Electoral College. The Electoral College was designed as a balance of power measure for states that have less population than others. The thought was that a presidential candidate would need to have broad political appeal to win using the Electoral College system. States with smaller populations would be just as important as larger states because they were needed to acquire the votes necessary to win the majority.

Side note, slavery played a major part in this. Southern states argued that although slaves could not vote, they still should provide some political representation for the South. Southern framers argued that states where slaves lived should have some political recognition for the population of the non-voting members of that state. A compromise was worked out were three-fifths of that state's total slaves' population would be counted when comprising the House of Representatives. This provided a huge political advantage for the South. Even though the South had fewer free-voting members then Northern states, they still had more political power in the House. They were using slaves for political power while still holding them as subjects. More hypocrisy, but I digress.

Within the current application of the Electoral College system, there are states that consistently vote Democratic and states that consistently vote Republican. With certain states, there is no uncertainly whatsoever. We know these states will vote either red or blue. During each election cycle, we know states like Alaska, Wyoming, Montana, and Utah will vote Republican.

States like New York, California, Hawaii, and Illinois will always vote Democratic. States that are less certain and that could vote for either party are called swing states. Some cycles, these states vote for one party, next election they vote for the opposition. States such as Pennsylvania, Wisconsin, and Arizona have all voted for both a Democrat and Republican for president within the last three election cycles. These states are the battleground that determines the outcomes of presidential elections.

The size of some Democratic Electoral College strongholds is massive. This is especially true in California and New York where California has 55 votes and New York has 29. The largest Republican stronghold is the state of Texas where there are 38 votes that, throughout recent history, have been solid red.

Demographics are changing, however, and Texas is becoming more and more competitive. If current trends continue, within the next few years, Texas will switch from a solidly Republican state to a battleground. This provides an opportunity.

The Covid-19 pandemic had huge impacts on our economy, our labor markets, and the view on work itself. In March 2020, when many governments mandated stay-at-home orders, this forced society to reimagine the traditional work dynamic. This led to a re-thinking of how work can be performed and the space in which it needed to be completed. Remote work became essential to our new existence and became the way in which many employees completed their duties and tasks.

In the initial stages of the pandemic, unemployment hit record highs and the economic turmoil of the shutdowns hurt many employers. Later, however, during the recovery from it, the labor markets were able to rebound to where our economy had record numbers of available positions open to be filled. Unemployment at this moment was at record lows.

This created a huge demand for workers and employers aggressively tried to fill their open positions. This created huge advantages for workers in terms of higher pay, more flexibility, and better working conditions.

The dynamics of this situation have created a window we can use to force political compromise. I propose that we strongly consider deconcentrating Democratic voters in urban population centers that are Democratic-stronghold states. If individuals have the ability to work remotely and the financial capacity to relocate, it would be of political advantage to do so. If these individuals could move to states that lack Democratic voices, this would challenge the current political composition. More specifically, adding more Democratic voters to the states of Texas, Arizona, and Georgia would change the political landscape.

Imagine if thousands of progressive tech workers located in San Francisco would consider relocating to Austin, Savannah, or Sedona. These workers could choose not just to move to the larger urban areas in these communities, but also to rural and suburban areas as well. With New York and California solid blue, a Democrat winning Texas, Arizona, and Georgia would lock the Electoral College for the Dems. The hope would be that with an influx of Democratic voters, these states would now become toss-ups and not solid red during election cycles. This would reprioritize moderate voices who appeal to some on the right and some on the left instead of those who speak to the extreme.

Politicians would have to speak to the center because they would need votes from both sides in order to win the state. In addition to refocusing on moderate ideology, hopefully this redistribution of voters would impact gerrymandering. There would be less desire to create structural demographic advantages because more voters of different political ideologies are spread across different spaces.

Common-like voters are not as concentrated. There is also the
thought that moderate politicians would be able and more
willing to work with their political opposition to get things
done and compromise politically to lead the community they
were elected to represent.

I know these recommendations are huge. They are
major things to consider. However, we are at a point when we
are going to need major action in order to move forward. We
must find a way to compromise politically. If it is not with the
recommendations that I just provided, there has to be some
movement and actions that will allow this to happen. It is
critical to our survival. If we are unable to make progress in
this fight, we will have troubling days ahead of us. We have to
be smart in the manner in which we act. Tearing the entire
house down will not work. Our protest movements need a
healthy democracy in order to have any impact. We need the
system to survive in order to end our experience of injustice
within it.

Chapter 8

Rage

No Justice, No Peace.
-Community Attributed

There was a time a few years back where I recall watching one of my favorite sports network analysts on one of my favorite sports network morning shows. This analyst's name was Bomani Jones and I thought his perspective was always a breath of fresh air. Bomani, along with Jemele Hill and a few others, was a textbook example of unapologetic black intellectualism and charisma that I was happy to see on a national platform.

I think that both Bomani and Jemele were very gifted at breaking down complex issues and bluntly speaking truth in a space where so much nonsense is allowed to reign free. To put another way, they are going to provide their audience with blunt truths that aren't altered just because what they are saying may be uncomfortable to some. They are going to speak their truth, regardless of your opinions, and they will do so unapologetically.

On this particular morning, Bomani was an on-camera guest for the network and he caused an uproar by the attire he decided to wear on the show. Bomani appeared on camera with a T-shirt that was made to look like the logo of the Cleveland Indians baseball team. Instead of the person of Native American descent, with the darker skin complexion that is common for a person of that decent, wearing a War Bonnet and the word "Indians" above the image, Bomani's shirt contained a re-designed image. Bomani's shirt had a white male as the central image of the shirt. The feather of the War Bonnet was replaced with a dollar sign. Finally, the "Indians" now read "Caucasians."

I thought this was perfect. This moment gave me much satisfaction and provided so much humor for me. The irony of the shirt was just perfect; it truly hit the mark.

For many years, many have been calling for the Cleveland Indians, the Washington Redskins, the Atlanta Braves, and a few others to change their team name. People have lobbied behind the scenes, there has been public pressure, and there have been many other lobbying efforts to get the teams to change the name.

Unfortunately, for years and years these efforts have been unsuccessful. Time and time again, Cleveland would comment that they did not find the name to be disrespectful or insensitive.

The fact that many of these lobbying efforts were coordinated and originated by people of Native American decent meant nothing. The team was steadfast in its position that the name was socially acceptable.

Not only were they okay with the team name, so were the hundreds of business partners who did business with the Cleveland Indians and all of the other teams mentioned. They're willingness to partner, advertise, market, and televise the product of the team shows complicity that cannot be overlooked. Remember the central theme of the *Staying Woke is Killing Me* series – oppression and racism are dichotomous. Either you are actively fighting against it or you are complicit. There is no middle ground, no gray area. Period.

So obviously the host of the show immediately asked Bomani about the shirt and about the point he was trying to make. To me the point was pretty obvious, but the host needed to hear Bomani verbalize his commentary. To Bomani's credit, he made the strategic decision to not provide too much context on the shirt. He was simple in his explanation of the shirt saying at first that the shirt was clean and that he liked the shirt. He also thought that it was funny and that it was exactly like the Cleveland Indians shirt. He also stated that many people have not taken issue with the Cleveland Indians logo and those shirts were socially accepted. The same should go for his.

So, throughout the morning, I am seeing him make appearances on camera with this shirt and I am finding more and more hilarious the discomfort that his shirt causing many who are on the air with him. By this time, Twitter is blowing up in controversy about the shirt as well. Not so hard to believe, there is outrage at him and at the network for allowing him to wear the shirt.

It is at this point in my mind when I begin the countdown clock. I know that sooner rather than later, network executives are either going to pull him from the air or ask him to change his attire. I was correct. In the middle of a commercial break for one of his appearances, Bomani was wearing a sweatshirt that was fully zippered to cover the shirt. Executives at the network asked him to cover the shirt up. They said to him that he had made his point and it was time to change his appearance.

My initial reaction was satisfaction. I looked at the Twitter posts from disgruntled users and I watched Bomani sitting on set with the fully zippered sweatshirt and was quite pleased by what he was able to accomplish. However, my feelings of humor and satisfaction quickly changed to what they commonly do – rage.

Bomani's point was quite sensible. It was very hard to deny his logic. For years, the Indians team name was allowed to survive and be a huge source of revenue for many people. Commerce was generated using that image despite the constant outcries of individuals who felt the image was insensitive at least and more than likely racist. Why was his shirt an issue for the network, yet the network had no problem broadcasting the team logo? It was at that moment when I realized the sad truth. Bomani was asked to change his appearance because he made people, mainly white people, feel uncomfortable. This was yet another moment when the outcome of a situation was dictated by the comfort of white individuals.

The rage that I felt in that moment was palpable. The irony of being asked to change something because it offends white people while not acknowledging the ignorance of the source material was absolutely infuriating. For many people, there was absolutely no issue with Chief Wahoo for years, but the moment something makes the white mainstream culture uncomfortable, there is an immediate issue.

Time and time again in this society, it appears that movements and reactions are based on white convenience and not the facts that we all see with our own eyes and the realities that the oppressed are forced to face in their lives.

Eventually, Cleveland changed their name to the Guardians after the 2021 season. Team leadership communicated that the killing of George Floyd in the summer of 2020 spurred intention to change the team's name. Although this was the right decision to change the team's name, it is very frustrating that this change did not happen sooner. It was yet another reminder that, with the way society is currently structured, no change will happen until it is authorized by the powerful. And this is what pisses me off the most. Things are only okay when "they" say that they are okay. With the construct of our current life, the ruling class says when, where, and how change is allowed to happen. This is infuriating.

2020 was obviously a difficult year for many of us. We were forced to navigate life in a global pandemic. Things changed drastically for all of us as we made intense changes and uprooted our lives in an effort to survive. Covid-19 changed life as we know it and caused much pain, suffering, and devastation throughout the world.

Not only were we forced to deal with the pandemic caused by Covid, we also lost more and more lives to racism and police brutality. Ahmaud Arbery was murdered in Georgia by three white men as he was jogging unarmed. Breonna Taylor was murdered in her own apartment as police charged into her home firing shots toward her and her boyfriend. And the world watched in absolute horror as we lost George Floyd.

The murder of George Floyd was one of the most painful things a lot of us had ever seen. The way in which he died was devasting. He did not deserve the agony and destruction he was confronted with. His murderer knelt on his neck for more than eight minutes without any regard. He did so with the understanding that he was being filmed and that there was literally a crowd watching his actions, pleading for George's life.

There was power that his murderer believed he had that was socially conditioned by society. This was something that many of us had seen before. Often that power was used toward others and it destroyed many other lives, often without consequence. Seeing the life snatched from another individual is a traumatizing event to watch. The entire world was forced to deal with this trauma. Because of the brutality of this experience, the nation was forced to stand up and pay attention.

In the death of George Floyd, we saw that entire murder happen on camera. He was killed while unarmed and defenseless. The murder of George Floyd sparked uprisings throughout the nation. His loss galvanized the world. Maybe it was the video. Maybe it was his cries for help. Maybe it was the clear and absolute viciousness of the police officer that was hard for many to accept. Whatever the catalyst, his story sparked mass public response.

People took action. People took to the streets. People demanded change. Protests happened not only here in America but all throughout the world. During these protests, individuals demanded justice and vowed to join the fight to end racism. Fortune 500 companies took on the mantra that Black Lives Matter, a statement that for many was met with continuous opposition. Pro athletes, both black and white, boycotted and demanded action on social justice. This was a moment where I felt like the world stepped up and stepped in and said no more. Enough is enough.

Watching these protests and demonstrations of solidarity, I felt plenty of emotions. First, there was pride. I was tremendously proud of society in that moment. The actions at that moment were public recognition that many live in injustice and that action needed to be taken to ensure that injustice will no longer continue. It seemed like the Rainbow Coalition that Fred Hampton died trying to create was continuing its formation. For once, it seemed like the masses were finally on our side and was committed to taking action toward the demise of injustice.

However, as with a lot of things in my experience, that pride was soon met with internal turmoil. This internal turmoil led to my next emotion – confusion. As happy and prideful as I was in seeing that call to action happening right in front of my eyes, there was one constant thought that ran over and over in my mind. Simply put, why now?

Violence, police brutality, and racial discrimination have been clearly evident for years in this country. The late great John Lewis, who also passed in 2020 at the age of 80, was beaten within an inch of his life on Bloody Sunday. His assault happened in front of news outlets that broadcasted those images for the world to see. The nation and the world witnessed that horror.

He was 25 when that happened. That was over 50 years ago, yet we are still fighting that same oppression. That moment all those years ago was also supposed to be a turning point, a moment where things were supposed to change, yet we still carry this burden of oppression.

Is it right to question the motives of those who are standing in solidarity? Should we, as a community of the oppressed, just be grateful that individuals are willing to stand with us in this fight? Or should we challenge their motives and ask why they are doing so? Why did so many go into the streets during the Summer of 2020?

Why did so many companies release messages for calls of social justice during that summer? What were their intentions and were they pure? What is the motivation of those with privilege who are now active in this fight? Is this the conscience of society that is motivating people to act? Or is this the guilt that is carried for all the past injustice? Or maybe it is the fear of the public shaming that will happen if individuals do not participate.

It is important that we know the motivating factors of what is causing society to act now, in this moment because we needed them previously. We needed these allies before the summer of 2020. Think of the impact that could have been made if so many people stood up in the same manner that they did during this moment. We have been dealing with this pain for generations, and although gaining new allies is very appreciated, the opportunity was there for them to join beforehand. Why is now the moment in which they have decided to become active in this fight?

I understand the questioning of motives can cause resentment among those who are looking to help. Please understand that is not the goal. However, this information is needed so that we can begin to build a rapport with our new allies and understand their level of commitment to this fight.

It is important that we know the depth of their conviction and hear that their participation will not ebb and flow with the trends of popular culture. We need to know that they are with us for a reason and plan on staying with us until we eliminate the injustice that exists within society.

And once we get these answers, it is important that we welcome our new members with open arms. It is natural to be skeptical, however, we cannot let that stop us from adding a member who is willing to fight alongside of us. A person joining this fight is taking a huge step outside of their normal experience. Because of their privilege, they have the ability to stay on the sidelines.

By joining our coalition, they are acknowledging that privilege does exist and they are committed to ending it. Because they have the opportunity to benefit from it, when they join our team, they are taking action to eliminate something that could be used for their own self-interest. Despite our feelings of resentment that they had this privilege in the first place, we must acknowledge that their actions in this fight demonstrate a willingness to sacrifice something they could benefit from. Just as they are willing to now stand with us, we must show that we also are standing with them. Together, we are in this fight.

It will take this level of deep understanding to strengthen our bond as a community and build trust with one another. And it will take that trust to move past what is so commonly felt by so many living with injustice – rage.

Just as constant as the ruling class's dominance of society is the rage that the oppressed have felt because of it. That rage is evident throughout our daily experience and is visible in our response to the injustice that we have always faced. It was visible during that same summer of 2020. While millions across the world protested using non-violent measures, other individuals did not.

Some of the uprisings that took place during 2020 were not peaceful. The outpouring of emotion led to property being destroyed throughout many cities where these protests were happening. If I am being honest, there was a part of me that did not feel bad about it. In fact, I understood it. At my core, I understood the motivations of those who chose to engage in those destructive actions. Systemic oppression is structural and progresses with assumed and expected behavior. Capitulation only furthers the oppression. So fuck it, let's take the unexpected position. Let's respond in a way that makes the population feel uncomfortable, that makes them feel it. Let them see the pain, let them see the anger.

Or, to put it another way, I will quote the words of Kimberley Jones, a brilliant activist who went viral for a speech she made during the Atlanta uprisings. She passionately articulated this speech in response to the destruction of property that happened in that community. She stated;

"So when they say, 'Why do you burn down the community? Why would you burn down your own neighborhood?' It's not ours. We don't own anything. There is a social contract that we all have. That if you steal or if I steal, then the person who is the authority comes in and they fix the situation, but the person who fixes the situation is killing us. So the social construct is broken. And if the social contract is broken, why the fuck do I give a shit about burning the Football Hall of Fame? About burning a fucking Target? You broke the contract when you killed us in the streets and didn't give a fuck. You broke the contract for 400 years. We played your game and built your wealth. You broke the contract when we built our wealth, again on our own bootstraps in Tulsa, and you dropped bombs on us.

When we built it in Rosewood and you came through and you slaughtered us. You broke the contract, so fuck your Target. Fuck your Hall of Fame. As far as I'm concerned they can burn this bitch to the ground. And it still would not be enough. And they are lucky that what black people are looking for is equality and not revenge."

And that's it. That's the anger. That's the pain felt by so many, a feeling that is just always there. Part of being an adult is learning how to manage and to stay in control of your emotions. However, how do you do so when what you feel most consistently is rage?

What you feel is anger because of the inequality you face and the privilege that others have that you do not. In my journey, this rage is always with me, and I have to restrain myself from indulging in it.

Day in and day out, I work on myself so that I do not give in to it and I do not act impulsively or emotionally because of the constant state of rage that I feel. I know where that road leads. Eventually, that road leads to violence and destruction. That's not the answer. Dr. King once said that violence only begets more violence. Although it feels very gratifying in the moment, violence, destruction, and aggression ultimately do not provide the type of response that is needed to get the desired outcome that we seek.

Instead of destructive means, we must try to channel this rage constructively. Our best path forward is to seek solidarity and seek to unite communities in support of the struggle. The more we can educate individuals, hopefully the more people will understand the injustice that many of us are forced to deal with. After seeing this and understanding what exactly is happening, hopefully people will continue to mobilize and take action to end it.

Hopefully, we can use our experience to gain an ally, a new member in the fight to eliminate oppression. We must take that rage and find ways to repurpose it for that goal. Try to use that emotion to create allies, not to harden opposition.

In Volume One, we spoke about the reality that oppression is dichotomous. It is a black and white issue where there is no gray area. It's something that either you are actively fighting against or an issue that you are actively contributing to. Silence does not absolve you of responsibility. Inactivity does not reprieve you of responsibility. Sitting on the sidelines is just as harmful as a person who is taking intentional action to oppress others.

As inhabitants of this society, my core belief is that we have an obligation to one another. We are required to treat each other with respect and to look out for the people we share this society with. We are also required to do the right thing in service of our neighbors. From this perspective, we all have an obligation to fight oppression. We all are required to fight inequality.

For the oppressed, we have a duty to fight past the pain, to fight past the rage. I know this can be a difficult thought to comprehend, but we must persist. In my previous work, I talk at length about the emotional turmoil that exists just by being conscious of my own oppression in today's society. It simply is an emotional struggle to be Black and Woke in America. Not only do I have to deal with the emotional struggle, I also have a constant internal battle happening in my spirit about what exactly to do with those feelings. There is a part of me that feels that my life would have been simpler, maybe somewhat easier, if I was unaware of my oppression. Yes, the oppression would still exist, however, I would be ignorant to it, so maybe my life would be an easier burden.

I have come to now realize that was the wrong position to take. Mostly because, even if I were ignorant, injustice would just continue forward. And it would do so with one less person fighting against it. This cycle would never end. And how much peace can you have living unjustly? How happy would I be living with and accepting the burden of injustice?

Part of those feelings stem from the emotional turmoil of it all. The rage, the pain…that shit adds up. Those are heavy to carry constantly in your spirit. Peace and joy are desired for all of our hearts, but for me it seems those feelings are in a constant duel with everything else that I feel. Furthermore, there is also the feeling of not knowing exactly what to do with everything that I feel. What do I do with the emotions? What is the best plan to fight the oppression?

Throughout history, there have been multiple organized movements of opposition in the fight for racial equality. History has shown us multiple approaches for how to move forward as a community to eliminate racial injustice. Systemic oppression has always plagued society and the victims of it have tried to resist and fight against it for years on end.

For years, the community orchestrated a campaign and movement that was based on civil disobedience and non-violence. That civil disobedience and non-violence was met with coordinated and state-sanctioned terrorism that viciously targeted so many communities of color. Those individuals that beat John Lewis within an inch of his life on that bridge on Bloody Sunday? Yeah, those were state troopers who delivered that beating.

Transitioning from that movement, there was a time when many within the community joined an armed resistance. The foundation of that movement was not grounded in violence; it was based on self-defense.

The idea was not that the community would arm themselves to be violent aggressors who would attack other communities without cause. The idea was that these individuals would arm themselves to defend themselves from the years of unprovoked attack that has been directed toward them and their community. The premise was that if you punch me, I am going to punch you back. If you shoot at me, I am going to shoot right back at you. Basically, the days of turning the other cheek were finished. They did not want violence, did not provoke violence, but made the decision to organize, strategize, and train their members. If attacked, they were prepared to respond in their defense with the same level of force that they were attacked with.

However, just like with the civil disobedience movement, the Black Panther movement was met with significant resistance and coordinated terrorism and violence. In both circumstances, leaders from these movements were assassinated because they were seen as a threat. Many leaders were surveilled, harassed by state and the federal government, and eventually murdered because of what they represented.

So, when you examine this landscape, you are able to see the full scope of resistance that has been tried by the people in response to this oppression.

One side of the scope is a non-violent response, the other side a violent response. Despite the stark differences in approach, you see that both were met with the same outcome – violence, murder, and overwhelming dominance from the ruling class.

What does this show? It shows that the powerful have no desire to relinquish their power. The core issue is not the manner in which oppression is being responded to. The core issue is that it's being challenged at all.

This is something that the powerful have to come to terms with. They have to come to terms with releasing the power that they cling to and wield over the marginalized. It is in their best interest to help society transition to a place where oppression no longer exists.

One of the arguments that I consistently communicate is that the continued systemic oppression of a group of people leads to one inevitable outcome – revolt. The oppressed will not continue to live in an unjust status quo. Eventually they will rise up and overthrow their oppressors. As activist Kimberlie Jones stated, right now, what the community is looking for is equality and not revenge. That can change overtime. If this dominance continues to reign supreme, eventually this relationship will deteriorate into vengeance and retaliation in response to the years of pain suffered from the oppressed. We do not want to see that, because at that point it will be too late.

I know this may all seem very abstract. However, we must prepare ourselves. This could very well happen. Time and time again, one great society after another has fallen because it did not address this core issue. America is no different. We need to pay attention and we need to take action to address this. To reiterate an earlier point, this is literally how this country started. The American revolutionaries, tired of the oppression of British rule, declared themselves a free and independent nation. Then they took up arms to win their freedom. With that as the foundation of the nation, we have to acknowledge this society can fracture if oppression remains a continued part of it.

Democracy is fragile and has to be protected. The continued dominance by one group of people suffocates a democracy and presents real challenges. Democratic societies have to feel as though they are representing the will of the people, not just the will of a few. This is what our current system feels like. The group of individuals who have power are able to control what the nation looks and feels like. Those who do not belong to this group do not get a say in the direction of our society. The oppressed feel like outsiders in their own land. This cannot continue. Eventually this will catch up to us. It is inevitable.

While highlighting the existence of oppression, I do not want to paint the picture that we have not made progress in this fight. There has been change. We have won some battles in this war that we are fighting. There have been gains that those outside of the ruling class have made. However, despite that progress, oppression still exists. No matter the circumstances, in this country the powerful continue to dominate the disenfranchised. That is the through line that is ever present within our nation. And despite that progress, we continue to cycle through this same illness that is plaguing our society.

My fear now is that as society evolves, the gains made have now become a representation of the power the ruling class still has within this society. There are moments of recognition that are used to showcase change, but do not address the structural mechanisms that keep the oppressed relegated to the lower classes.

African-American unemployment was at all-time lows before the Covid pandemic. However, student debt and barriers to home ownership doesn't provide the community opportunities to build wealth and truly get ahead. Society celebrates trans citizens during Pride month while government systematically blocks access to medical care for so many within the community.

The more things like this continue, the more our society is being torn apart. We are a modern society that has evolved over time but one that still carries wounds from our past. We are not learning from those past failures, while continuing to traumatize current society and sabotage our future.

We have to pay attention. There is a parallel that is undeniable between the images of our past and our current society. When I look at the protests from 2020, I see the similarities in the protests of the 1960s. When I see Tamir Rice, I also see Emmitt Till. These are protest movements and victims of the same oppression that has plagued our nation for years.

I understand that it is difficult to hold individuals responsible for things they are unaware of. There could be individuals who are unaware of the challenges that many of their neighbors face, not because of a lack of concern, but due to a lack of exposure. With the access to information that we currently have, it seems unlikely, but it could be possible. This is where those of us who are informed come in to fill that void. It is our job to educate and to explain these issues to those who have been privileged enough to just not know.

For the rest of us, however, those who know and understand these issues, we are responsible for the next steps we must take as a community. Knowledge comes with the mandate of accountability. To know and to not act is to be complicit in the oppression. The complicity of good and honest people is a large part of what has enabled oppression to continue for as long as it has. This is a weakness within our current makeup. This is our failure that we must correct.

And if we do not take these steps, if we do not act, what comes next will be our own doing. We have the opportunity to understand that we have a problem we can still do something about.

There is something very American about knowing we have an issue and still not addressing it. There are multiple things currently plaguing society that we simply refuse to address. Oppression is not the only thing that is tearing this nation apart. And the more we do not address these issues, the closer we are to our undoing. We have to find the courage to find our way back to a more cohesive place. We have to find a place that is loyal to our collective wellbeing and not solely dedicated to our own self-interest.

So what does this look like? We spent the last chapter talking about how we should act, but first we have to make the decision to act. We have to make the first move. We have to make the internal decision that this is not okay and dedicate ourselves to changing things in our community. After we have arrived at that space, we then should focus on acquiring as much knowledge on these issues as possible. If this is your first time reading about oppression, discrimination, and injustice, I am proud of you for taking this step. Continue forward in your journey and share the knowledge you gain with someone who may not know about what you are learning.

For those who are well-versed in this material, it is our duty to lead and to contribute. As discussed in the last chapter, the actions that we take must be strategic and must be full of purpose. And for individuals like myself, we cannot be consumed so much by our rage that we do not take action that will enable change. Just as we demand the powerful relinquish their dominance, we have to sacrifice our desire to isolate or retaliate because of our anger. And this is coming from someone who looks at society and is pretty damn mad. We have to move forward in a positive manner that builds and does not destroy.

We also must stay engaged. I know at times I have considered trying to ignore oppression to have some type of peace. I have also considered isolating to a community that is only populated by individuals who share the same experience and who will not hurt me. As much as a safe space I think that will be, it does not protect those who are without that space to retreat to. It does not change the circumstances of the community that I am committed to. It just banishes me to a bubble of emotional protection, where I am not willing to sacrifice my peace for progression.

We have to fight this. We must do so with the understanding that the burden that this comes with is heavy. At times, the burden felt having to explain this reality to those who don't understand can be overwhelming. This is something in which I have personal experience. It's a feeling of constant responsibility, a realization that you represent so much more than just yourself. On one hand, it's a thrill to connect with someone who wants to learn and find ways they can best help. But on the other hand, it now becomes your responsibility to educate and represent an entire people and culture just to gain an ally for equality, that same equality that the person you are explaining your experience to was provided at birth with no struggle or expectation of it not being there for them. This is truly difficult. Honestly, some days I don't want to be the explainer for an entire community. Some days I don't want to serve as an oppression translator. Some days I just want to be myself. I just want peace.

In the first chapter, we talked about how we need the recognition of the hypocrisy to begin the process of healing. However, we as a community will not have complete peace until society changes. Absolute healing without societal change is not possible.

So, I press forward. I continue the fight to make that change. There comes a moment when we all have to question ourselves and see what our level of commitment is. When this moment comes, empty rhetoric and symbolic gestures mean nothing. This requires action. How are you willing to contribute? What steps do you think would be best for you to take? What is your plan to impact society? How will you help create this change that we desperately need?

As I said multiple times now, once you hear something, once you learn something, you are now accountable for it. Through these pages, I give every reader a charge: You must get involved. You must participate in this struggle against oppression. Society needs to change. We need you to be a part of that change.

Our democracy is in trouble. Big trouble. This is a moment for our nation that makes me very afraid because I see the cracks widening in the foundation of our society. Despite my fear, I remain very confident that we have what it takes to fix this. We can right this ship. Together as a society, we have the ability to do what is required to fix the brokenness and division that we are falling deeper and deeper into. The question is are we willing to do what is necessary to fix our current reality and transition to a different space?

It would be a tragedy if we let it all fall apart, if we give into our anger, if we are blindly driven by impulse and rage. It will be tragic if the powerful remain selfish and do not make concessions to change dynamics within society. Just as we have the responsibility to fight, they have the responsibility to learn, listen, and act. And they must understand that a concession of their power is in their best interest. In the short term, yes, they will lose their dominance, but it protects them in the long term. The only other alternative is a complete fracture of society, which will leave them targeted when society collapses. And please understand, unless we make changes, the collapse is sure to come.

History has shown us time and time again, that great societies, no matter how powerful, can fail. We have to be willing to do what is necessary to protect our Union. This is part of the work. This is what is necessary. Both the powerful and the oppressed have things that we need to do to ensure that we continue forward in a totally new space. That we move toward the dawn of a new day where injustice no longer exists. It is possible to achieve this. We are responsible for getting to work to make this happen.

Acknowledgments

God- I am grateful to be a child of yours. Thank you for your grace, your love, and for also guiding my path. All that I am is because of you. I give YOU all the glory, honor, and praise.

Linda, Darnell Sr, Darnell Jr. Our family is not perfect. Nothing in this realm is. But the bond of love that we share is as close to perfection that we can get. Thank you for loving me wholly and completely. Just the way that I am.

Annex Crew. One of God's greatest gifts was placing each of you in my life. Blood cannot make us any closer. You all are my family. A true blessing that I do not deserve, but I am so grateful to have. I love each of you.

Eb. This project would not have happened without the 2-3 hour processing sessions on these topics. Words cannot fully express my gratitude. Thank you for your unwavering support and your constant encouragement to always be myself.

Monica. Editing is a tough job. Thanks for your willingness to work with me on this series. Most importantly, thanks for your guidance, encouragement, and kindness. It truly helps me reach the finish line.

ODAAT Team. Working alongside of you is an honor of a lifetime. Thanks for being my partners in service.

Society. Thank You for allowing me to serve.

NOTES

NOTES

NOTES

NOTES

NOTES

MORE FROM THE AUTHOR:

Staying Woke is Killing Me, Vol. 1, Available now!